Tails I Lose

Tails
I Lose

Coping with Bird Dogs

Joel M. Vance

THE DERRYDALE PRESS
Lanham and New York

THE DERRYDALE PRESS

Published in the United States of America
by The Derrydale Press
4720 Boston Way, Lanham, Maryland 20706

Distributed by NATIONAL BOOK NETWORK, INC.

First Derrydale Printing 2000

Library of Congress Cataloging-in-Publication Data

Vance, Joel M., 1934-
    Tails I lose : coping with bird dogs / by Joel M. Vance.
    p. cm.
    ISBN 1-58667-034-4 (cloth : alk. paper)
    1. Bird dogs—Missouri—Biography. 2. Human-animal relationships—Missouri. 3.
Vance, Joel M., 19334- I. Title.

SF428.5.V26 2000
799.2'34—dc21   00-029033

This book is dedicated to the people at Stover Publications, especially retired editor Bob Wilbanks, present editor Rick Van Etten, and owner Roger Stover, for letting me rant in a *Gun Dog* magazine conservation column for nearly twenty years and for giving me space to tell dog stories there and in a companion magazine, *Wing and Shot*.

Thanks also to Dave Follansbee, the first editor at *Gun Dog*, who introduced me to the wonders of French Brittanies and arranged for me to be owned by a puppy named McGuffin du Calembour.

My thanks and my love go to our son Andy Vance, co-owner and trainer of the Vance dog dynasty and my hunting partner since he was the same height and weight as a bird dog.

And most of all my love and eternal appreciation to Marty Vance, who was appalled but resigned when her husband pleaded for a traditional brace of Brittanies and who now must put up with several braces of them, plus the same husband.

CONTENTS

Introduction

There is a wonderful line in the movie *E.T.* when Everett, the little boy/hero, looks at one of his friends who is romanticizing the great adventure and says, "This is reality, Herbie!"

I have a library of great sporting writing, shimmering prose ranging from the gaudily turgid to the gloriously uplifting. Only rarely does it rain in those pages. Only rarely does the author speak of numbed fingers, a nose that dribbles like a rusty tap, guns that speckle before your eyes with oxidation, dogs shivering and stinking, with torn nails and cut paws.

Who wants to read junk like that anyway?

If the random author does drag sleet into his prose like a dead cat, it's only to set the stage for a description of how he subsequently shot the biggest buck ever taken in them parts.

Chances are he will urge you, too, to get out in foul weather so you can duplicate his feat. Resist this urge.

Shiver delicately and put your hands to the warming fire because all you will find out there is sleet, much of it running down the back of your neck. Any buck with brains enough to grow a forked antler of any size is holed up in stuff so dense you couldn't part it with a D-7 Caterpillar.

The reality of the outdoors is a runny nose. When you stand reverently before a Robert Abbett painting, you see a sun-shot scene of a lanky bird hunter at a small stream, a Brittany staunch on point, as a woodcock rises into the evening light. The hunter is mounting his gun, preparatory to dumping that bog sucker on his feathered bumper.

Translate this tender scene into reality, a day in northern Minnesota that is not cold enough to drop a scenic snow (which Chet Reneson would paint, with a few bluebills dropping to the blocks). No, it's just above freezing and it's raining. The insistent rain is punctuated by spits of sleet. In this sleety scene we see a hunter who is anything but lanky ("lardassed" is a pejorative that has been uttered). He huddles in "water resistant" foul-weather gear, which means that the gear resisted the water for about three seconds.

If the hunter and his dog fill the game bag that day, it will be by picking up grouse and woodcock that have succumbed to exposure.

His Brittany trudges mechanically ahead of him, in sullen misery. The dog is thinking of his warm kennel, filled food dish, and cozy bunkmates. He also is thinking of attacking his master with claw and fang. Even though the hunting instinct burns like molten lava in this dog, there are times when lava cools and becomes gritty and hard.

Retribution is likely, for this is a dog that believes in getting even. He has done it before and he will do it again. This is the same Brittany that decorated me twice with critical moisture. For Guff and me both, this is reality in hunting.

Fishing is not much better. I learned to backlash almost before I could read the throbbing prose of Lefty Kreh or Dave Whitlock telling how a fly line should describe an elongated s as sinuous and lovely as a Metropolitan ballerina.

My cast? It resembles the symbols seen on pornographic movie theater marquees: XXX. Just tonight I loped down to the pond, fly rod in hand, with my last popping bug, to see the bluegills in a feeding frenzy. Never saw anything like it in our pond and never will again.

My first cast enticed a meaty tree limb thirty feet up; after an epic struggle the limb broke the leader.

Reality? Have you read about Theodore Gordon, dean of American fly fishermen? He tied his flies at streamside without a vise—a trick sort of like a cowpoke rolling a smoke with one hand while roping steers with the other or a sailor tying complex knots in string inside his mouth, using only his tongue.

If you would like to review the appearance of a fly tied by me, find a possum that has been centered by a Peterbilt. Once I tied dog hair streamers until the multicolored collie we owned at the time became hysterical every time he saw me with a pair of scissors and my wife made me leave him alone.

Reality is when the guide you hired at a price sufficient to enlist a mercenary major general to direct a Latin American revolution not only doesn't put you onto a single fish but catches a limit himself. This has happened to me twice. There is the slim possibility that I fish like the geriatrics ward plays jai alai, but on the other hand you'd think even a blind sow would trip over an acorn once in a while.

The last guide was horribly embarrassed as he hauled in smallmouth after smallmouth that looked like something off a bait shop taxidermy display. "Cain't understand it," he mooed sympathetically, grunting as he set the hook in yet another Master Angler fish. "Y'all oughta be catchin' just as many as me." He thought there was something wrong with the outboard until we realized the loud noise we heard was my teeth grinding.

I once fished for muskellunge with a biologist. He was casting what appeared to be a used telephone pole with painted eyes. He had a wire leader long and tough enough to bale most of a field of lespedeza and he recommended the same to me.

"A fable," I pontificated (using the same superior tone of voice that I had when the dog hosed me). "They almost never get the leader in their mouth . . ."

At that moment, a 42-inch muskellunge contributed to the delinquency of my minor league tackle and let me see him for an instant—as he closed his mouth over my 10-pound test. He grun (the past tense of "grin") and was gone.

I cried in anguish (and from the sleet), "Why me?" It may have been the wind howling, but I thought I heard a massive whisper from somewhere above me, "I don't know, Vance, there's just something about you that ticks me off."

The Associated Press once reported that authorities in Fyffe, Alabama, were puzzled by what they thought might be a flying saucer.

The police chief, Junior Garmany, and his assistant, Fred Works, said the object was hovering when they drove up to the scene of the report. "We got out of the car and we turned off the engine and the radio," said the chief. "When we started towards it, it began moving away."

Chief Garmany described the alien vehicle as "bigger than a jumbo jet" and covered with various colored lights and "going about three or four hundred miles an hour."

Another witness thought it looked like a banana with the arch upright.

But of all the witness reports, my favorite was from a Lickskillet, Alabama, resident who said, "You better get a deputy over here quick. I don't know what it is, but it's scaring the (expletive) out of my bird dogs."

I love that last paragraph. I love the name of the town. I'd give anything to live in a town called Lickskillet. You *have* to own bird dogs in a town like that.

I also know what expletive the UFO scared out of those dogs because I've often said that a bird dog is composed of one part dog, two parts waste material. If there is any creature that can create something from nothing, it is the bird dog. It is a form of alchemy, but it is not gold nuggets that Streak is depositing on your boss's new shell vest.

"DOG HAIKU"

I love my master;
Thus I perfume myself with
This long-rotten squirrel.

I lie belly-up
In the sunshine, happier than
You ever will be.

Today I sniffed
Many dog butts—I celebrate
By kissing your face.

I sound the alarm!
Paperboy—come to kill us all!
Look! Look! Look! Look! Look!

I sound the alarm!
Mailman fiend—come to kill us all!
Look! Look! Look! Look! Look!

I sound the alarm!
Meter reader—come to kill us all!
Look! Look! Look! Look! Look!

I sound the alarm!
Garbage man—come to kill us all!
Look! Look! Look! Look! Look!

I sound the alarm!
Neighbor's cat—come to kill us all!
Look! Look! Look! Look! Look!

I lift my leg and
Whiz on each bush.
Hello, Spot—
Sniff this and weep.

How do I love thee?
The ways are numberless as
My hairs on the rug.

My human is home!
I am so ecstatic I have
Made a puddle.

I hate my choke chain—
Look, world, they strangle me! Ack
Ack Ack Ack Ack Ack!

Sleeping here, my chin
On your foot—no greater bliss—well,
Maybe catching cats.

Look in my eyes and
Deny it. No human could
Love you as much I do.

The cat is not all
Bad—she fills the litter box
With Tootsie Rolls.

Dig under fence—why?
Because it's there. Because it's
There. Because it's there.

I am your best friend,
Now, always, and especially
When you are eating.

You may call them fleas,
But they are far more—I call
Them a vocation.

My owners' mood is
Romantic—I lie near their
Feet. I fart the big one.

ONE

Out There

A cold, sunny afternoon on a windy hillside in north Missouri. The countryside looks like something transplanted from North Dakota—rolling, grass-covered hills that billow to the horizon.

The three guys and the girl bound across the slope with energy scarcely slackened by five hours in the field. Me? I'm wearing lead chaps, pig iron boots. My hips ache; my feet hurt and the little double-barrel Browning weighs more than a pregnant sow.

There is a point. Chubby freezes in his characteristic crouch, as if he were trying to hide from whatever is in front of him. The other three skid to a stop, each in a distinctive attitude. Dacques is head-high, but his eyes are on Chubby. Tess is head-forward, her nose working to find the wonderful fug that has her big brother, Chubby, so enthralled. Flick, the new kid and nephew of the other three, hasn't really developed an intense point yet. He has stopped because somehow (not because of my sloppy training) he has developed manners and knows he is supposed to stop when everyone else does.

It is a snapshot in time. The golden light of late afternoon illumines the four dogs, their total immobility a contrast against the shimmering grass. The bird likely is a pheasant. If it's a rooster, it will probably run off, scooting through the knee-high grass with a sly lack of respect for the artistry of the dogs. I don't care if the pheasant runs off or not; this moment is too beautiful not to savor, and I stand for a long moment storing it in my mind before I walk in on them.

It's an anticlimax of sorts. The dogs trade point position as we follow the running bird up the hill. Now this dog, now that one goes on point and the others honor. Finally, far ahead, a hen pheasant flushes and flaps noisily to the distant bottom. The spell is broken. Maybe dramatic convention demanded that a noble rooster crouch in the grass and that I dump it in a frenzy of color . . . but bird hunting, like life, isn't always fair, nor perfect.

So we move on, looking for quail and pheasants. For the quartet of Brits, the lovely moment is gone. Bird dogs are tomorrow and tomorrow, and yesterday is a wisp of fog. But I won't forget it.

A brace of Brittanies is the standard measure, like a team of horses. Usually I hunt the dogs two by two, but this was the last day of a four-day hunt and we all were tamed by cumulative fatigue. The furious energy of the first day had given way to a persistent, not unpleasant ache. Snap-back time for gray panthers is longer than a good night's sleep.

But my son Andy, twenty-three, groaned and grumbled just like the rest of us, so maybe age isn't the determining factor. Maybe it's the trauma of six hours in the brush, being whipped by locust sprouts, abraded by blackberry, and twisted by clumps of prairie grass and hidden holes.

The dogs still burst from the kennel, but without the hysteria of opening day. And they wear down more quickly, so it's wise to hunt a pair in the morning and bring in the benchwarmers at noon. But we're leaving for home at noon, so why not turn the flock loose and see what happens. Four kennel mates in the field is a prescription for problems. Will they compete on points, bust birds? Will they, in their eagerness to be first in line, run through coveys? Will they be impossible to keep track of?

I use locator collars, but Dacques, the running back of the crew, has managed to rip the locator unit off one collar. Another collar is old and frail. I put the better one on Dacques, the fragile one on Tess. They're the runners, most apt to be hard to find.

Chubby and Flick are the best at checking back so if I don't see them every few minutes, it's time to go looking. You learn your dogs' strengths and weaknesses, like a coach with an athletic squad.

This is a new team, a new era. Chubby and Dacques are nine years old and graying at the muzzle. They still hunt with unbounded energy, but I'm sadly realistic. I know it can't go on much longer. Tess is three, their little sister three litters removed. They were from a first litter; Tess from a last litter six years later. Flick is the firstborn of Tess's sister.

So they're all of a family and, like a family, they bicker and grumble. But when they head into the field, all the petty squabbles are forgotten and we're in tune.

It has been a long haul with this Brittany regime. It stretches back to the time when I was young and death was something that happened to the stupid and the old.

Chip was my first bird dog.

Chip, a lust-driven American Brittany, vanished in the middle of the night, eddying in the irresistible wake of his in-heat kennel mate, Ginger. Two days later, he was killed by a car several miles from our home. His replacement was a French Brittany puppy, eight weeks old.

I named the puppy Guff, short for McGuffin. Still mourning for Chip, I wrote a letter to Guff which, as smart as he proved to be for the next dozen years, he would never read. But I would know . . .

Dear Pup:

I can feel your sweet breath tickling the hair on the top of my bare foot, down under the desk as I type. I guess I could just tell you these things, but then no one would know but us. When it's on paper it's somehow more permanent and meaningful. Spoken words go away and are forgotten.

You have big paws to grow into, little Brittany pup, but I have a feeling you'll do it. It has been almost a month since my best friend, Chip, was hit by a car, and I still have flashbacks when the tears well up and I can't swallow past the lump in my throat. I had one of those wrenching moments the first time you and I were alone.

Maybe you wondered why I hugged you so hard and buried my face in your soft coat. Well, it was because I miss so much the dog who shared so many seasons and so many miles with me. He wasn't the world's greatest bird dog. He made plenty of mistakes. He false pointed a lot and he wouldn't honor because he didn't like being second-best. He wasn't real fast and he probably didn't have the greatest nose on earth, but whatever bird you asked him to hunt he hunted and did pretty well at it. He had the heart of a lion. No water was too cold for him to plunge into and no brush was too thick for him to bust.

Only last year up in Iowa he chased a crippled pheasant into a bulldoze pile. He was squirmed so far down in the thick tangle of trees that all I could see was the tip of his tail and I feared he'd never get out. He was trying to chew through a four-inch tree trunk to get closer to the bird.

Chip was registered, but as far as I know he had no champions in his pedigree. You have a whole covey of them on both sides, bench and field. But can you endure heat and pollen in September and bitter cold in December, buck knee-high snow and shoulder your way endlessly through incredible tangles of vegetation, mile after mile, six or seven hours a day, and never once quit?

Chip did. He did it year after year, even after some deviate shot him with a .22 and left him unable to jump anymore. We thought he was going to be crippled in the hindquarters, but he healed and he galloped with a drunken sailor's rolling gait. It didn't matter. He'd drag himself over the blow downs he used to tiptoe over like a mountain goat. He never quit, little pup.

In a way I'm writing about you because you're the most beautiful little puppy I've ever seen. Elegant has to be the word, with a freckled face that would melt the hardest heart and clean body lines. You're already showing quick intelligence and that's why I think you're going to be the finest bird dog I've ever hunted behind. I swung a grouse wing past your nose the other day, holding a hand over your eyes, and you jumped as if I'd hit you with a cattle prod. That little black French Brittany nose quivered and flubbered with delicious shock. You were birdy, youngster, even if you didn't know what was happening to you.

And tonight I took you out in the country and we dropped a dove. I practically had to rub your nose in it, but when you finally caught the scent and spied it, you jittered and got what writer Bill Tarrant calls "boogery," and you picked it up by the tail and dropped it. A feeling was kicking around inside you, trying to tell you something. And the gunfire didn't even make you buck and snort. You look like a real comer to me, little Guff.

You're already coming to your name, Guff. It's a good, sharp, short call name, contracted from McGuffin. Wouldn't mean much to you, but it's what Alfred Hitchcock called the gimmick in his suspense movies—the thing that everyone was after. You'll have some fancy French name on your papers. It comes with the territory. Who cares? I don't even remember Chip's official name. He was just Chip or Chipper or a host of other names we made up as wordplays on Chip: "Lips," or "Lippy," because of his droopy jowls, for example. I seem to remember that's a fault for a Brittany in a bench show, but Chip couldn't have placed in the most amateurish Brittany bench show ever held. He was a bit cow hocked and fiddle fronted, and his eyes protruded too much and when you scolded him his ears flared out until he looked like a peeved elephant.

But you could roll an egg across the floor and he'd retrieve it without a scratch. I've seen crippled birds run right out of his mouth. He never once crunched one and that includes a big Canada goose, much more alive than dead, that put knuckle bumps all over Chip's head. Chip just squinched his eyes and kept on coming. But he was mighty glad to get rid of that bird. He had a golden mouth, that dog, dry and soft, and he loved to hunt for downed birds. He was a master at it.

God, I miss him, little pup! I wish . . . but wishes don't bring back old friends and crying never restored spilt milk to the bottle either. You're my new dog, Guffer, and it was love at first sight.

I heard you yowling in that little shipping cage out on the loading dock at the airport while I was trying to convince the surly functionaries inside that I wasn't going to stiff them for your shipping fee. Your little black eyes peered out through long cinnamon lashes, taking my measure, I thought. I hoped I'd pass the inspection.

Apparently I did, for you shot out of the cage and into our car and began licking and chewing Marty and me as if you were home at last and damned glad to be there. It has been the same since. You've settled into the household without a ripple. There's been no nighttime crying and you didn't even piddle on the floor a couple of nights. You're just swell, little guy and, as I said before, I fell in love with you instantly.

No, you're not Chip, but I don't resent you for that. I can love you as much and as fully as I did him, but I'll never forget him. He was the finest dog I've ever known. We shared everything. We shared tents in many an icy campground and, in the small hours when the cold became intense, I let him crawl shivering into the warm sleeping bag with me and we both benefited. A lot of nights it was one piece of popcorn for me, one for him. When I felt bad in the head, things going poorly, I could talk about it to Chip and lean my face against his and feel better for it. You can't tell me he didn't know I was down in the mouth. He didn't squirm or try to move away. He just leaned silently against me and maybe licked my ear, and if that wasn't sympathy, I don't know what is. Now it's up to you to do the same for me, little guy, and just now when I kind of broke up thinking about starting another hunting season without my pard, you roused and looked up at me and it was a soft look. Then you licked my hand when I knuckled your silky ears and stuck with me until I got over the worst of it.

Everyone who's lost someone dear wants to say something that will be memorable, that will express how much the relationship meant. But what we really want, Guffer, is to have them back and hold them close and say, "I'm so sorry for all the mean things I did and I love you with all my heart." That's the one thing that can't happen, though, so we make out as best we can with insufficient eulogies and cry our lonesome tears when no one is around.

I can see great times for us, Guff. Grouse hunts in Minnesota, pheasants in Iowa, quail in Missouri. Maybe a trip west to hunt some of those prairie grouse. Chip and I did that once. We went everywhere. He was a great traveler. I never knew he was in the car. His presence was only a big, sweet head on my thigh or amber eyes looking up at me from the floorboard on the passenger's side. But the minute the car door opened he shot out, ready to hunt, like a rodeo bucking horse—placid in the gates, hell in the arena.

You seem to be a good-humored little dog and that's fine. Chip always had a talent for the ridiculous and was involved in many of my fondest, funniest memories. Some day when I feel like laughing I'll tell you about those things. Some night when we're on the long road home from Iowa or Minnesota or somewhere and you're leaned up against me and the car lights flicker past, rifts of snow in the dark roadside ditches, I'll start to chuckle and you'll stir a bit and cock your head to listen and then I'll tell you.

Like the time when young Chip gobbled up a poinsettia leaf. We'd heard they were poisonous and were convinced he was doomed, so we tried to make him vomit by forcing warm salt water down him, in the backyard and in the teeth of a howling nor'wester. Chip never did vomit, though he was mightily peeved for a while. It was several years before I learned that a dog would have to eat about 600 poinsettia leaves to surpass a dose that had done absolutely no damage to a laboratory rat.

I'm not used to black noses and eyes on a dog. American Brittanies, you know, have red-rubber noses and amber eyes. So your little shoe-button nose and raccoon-bright eyes are something new and I think it'll be good for me. First of all, you have a wonderful face, cute now, but with lines that will turn you into real beauty when you're grown. Second, if you were Chip's twin, I'm afraid I'd forever be comparing you with him. And that wouldn't be fair to either of you.

It's getting late, little guy—late for me anyway, though not for you because you've been dozing for a long time now and probably will wake fully charged and ready for a romp about the time I'm ready for bed. I'm feeling kind of wrung out after this, so I hope you'll forgive me if I leave you with an old shoe and climb those stairs to bed. Old dreams and old friends, the faint click of familiar toenails on the floor now missing, the feel of a chunky soft-coated body next to mine . . . they drift off into the swirling current of time.

There are so many memories. I hope you realize how difficult this is, Guff. It really hurts. I guess I could total up the miles and the birds and all the sharp, clean moments for you so you can see what a big job you have ahead, but I don't think I could handle any more of that right now.

I hope, bit by bit, you'll do things that erase the big hurt and leave just the soft edges of Chip for me. Maybe your life will act as a counterbalance to the overwhelming sense of loss I've felt since I laid my hand on Chip's horribly still body and knew it was all over.

Well, little boy, this sure isn't getting us anywhere, picking at a scab barely formed. You're a feisty little stinker, with bristly courage and the genes of champions jiggling around in you. They tell me you're a can't-miss dog and besides that you're a charmer. I couldn't ask for anything more in a new dog.

So lie there and dream and twitch, maybe about that dove we shot together tonight.

We've got a long way to go together, pup.

TWO

The Lovely Moment

There are few upland bird hunters who say they go afield to kill a pile of birds. The shooting is incidental to the experience.

Much if not most of that experience is watching the dogs in action. Hunters without dogs are like the proverbial day without wine or sunshine or whatever it is. Dog work is so integral to the experience that it defines the sport. Being dogless is like playing air guitar.

I doubt the dogs have even a niggling of pride for me when I do something right in the field. They don't care what I do, just so I take them along to do it. Their excitement has no bounds when I load them up and shove gun and shell vest in the truck beside the portable kennels.

We've shared thousands of hours in the field, countless days. Every trip is special, but some are so special that they linger in the mind like lost loves. They are a bittersweet reminder of yesterday—sweet because they happened, bitter because they ended.

My mind is filled with memories. I can call up days when a dog performed so brilliantly as to bring tears to my eyes. I can also call up days when the performance brought words to my lips that would fuse asbestos.

Only a few times in a season, maybe in a lifetime, does everything come together to give the quail hunter a perfect day. Those days are as rare as rubies in a coal pile. Quail hunters, being the eternal optimists, dig through dung heaps, shouting, "With all this stuff there must be a pony in here somewhere!" And, sure enough, sometimes, a perfect little pony leaps out.

This was a pony day, or at least a pony afternoon. It hadn't started as a perfect day. The first part was less than ideal—in fact, it was downright awful. A branch jerked my shooting glasses off, the way branches do. (Branches are inventions of the devil; they get between your legs and trip you and they swat you on a cold cheek and they poke you in the eye if they can.)

The glasses went to glass heaven. They simply vanished. My son Andy and I looked for fifteen minutes for glasses that I knew had fallen at my feet; but if they did, they dug a hole and covered themselves up. Finally I wrote off the glasses and moved on, muttering imprecations. If I had been standing in front of a stainless steel wall saying the same things, it would have caught on fire.

Then Chubby decided to migrate to Mars. Chubby was nine years old and presumably a sedate, experienced bird dog. But once on every outing, he sticks his brain in his hip pocket and starts running; you couldn't flag him down with a rocket launcher. I saw him go over the hill about a half mile away and had visions of him flattened on the nearby highway. Brittanies have a suicide complex any-way—they will seek out a busy trafficway anywhere within a mile and stand in the middle of it, hoping to be whacked by one of Detroit's finest.

Chubby finally came back, after I had become so hoarse shouting for him that I sounded like Clint East-wood explaining the rules of life to bad guys. I wonder if Clint grew up with bird dogs. That could explain his hoarse voice and flinty eye.

So, to that point, things weren't so great. But the air temperature was just right—not too hot, a bite to the breeze. I function in hot weather the way an Adele pen-guin would function in Death Valley. This day was about thirty-five degrees, sunny, only a light breeze, the better to carry the ineffable stink of bird to the flubbering noses of Dacques, Chubby, Flick, and Pepper, the Vance Quartet.

The hunter crew included me and my son Andy, com-panion of twenty years. This was a Conservation Reserve Program farm, a mixture of crop fields and CRP-idled land, almost ten years into its set-aside mode. The prob-lem for quail is that the CRP acres have gone largely to grass, and quail are not grass critters.

They need annual seed-bearing weeds, which is what CRP offered the first three or four years. Now you find the birds using the grassy brush for cover, but they'll feed in the adjacent crop fields. After running a series of brushy draws with adjacent grass and striking out, we got smart and began to hunt the fringes of the crop fields . . . and began to find quail.

A perfect day for quail doesn't necessarily mean a perfect day shooting, though that's nice too. For me, dog work is 80 percent of quail hunting. Maybe 10 percent is walking unfamiliar country, feeling the tug of gravity on muscle and sinew, seeing what's on the land. You jump deer and turkeys (dogs are set back on their haunches when a turkey flushes instead of the little bird they're expecting; when quail get that big, you'd better watch out).

You see red-tailed hawks circling high and marsh hawks prowling low, and the occasional vole scurries out from under your boot—that's mostly why the hawks are there, though they wouldn't turn down a slow quail.

A local commented that if the government would loosen up and let them shoot hawks, there'd be a lot more quail. Not so—predators and prey have been having at it for eons and they still coexist. Government protection of red-tails doesn't mean fewer quail. The guy should have looked to the fall-plowed fields or the skinned-off fence rows or the bulldozed-in gullies or the grassed-over CRP. But that's all tougher to see than a circling hawk.

The final 10 percent of quail hunting is the shooting. A limit for me is a chimera, something that you read about in books by people who wore jodhpurs and tweed coats and hunted behind pointers named Old Bob. They've all been dead for half a century.

I know limit hunters and I refuse to admit they're any better shot than I am, the same way I refuse to admit that the reason I didn't start on our Keytesville basketball team was because I'm not very good.

So, anyway, this was a perfect day.

Chubby was back in the groove and Dacques, Pepper, and Flick were steady-on. Andy was my assistant gunner. Or, come to think of it, I was *his* assistant gunner, given comparative shooting statistics. There was a time when I played him and the neighborhood kid one-on-two in basketball and beat them handily. It embarrassed them and I would often see them practicing moves against each other that they hoped to use against me.

They grew older and I couldn't handle them one-on-two anymore, but I could still take Andy one-on-one and beat him handily. Then it was harder. Then he began to block my lazy moves. Then he began to block everything. Then I quit playing him.

We worked a broad, wooded gully from top to bottom, toward a distant bottom bean stubble field. We'd found in two previous days that quail were invariably near crop fields. The weather had been cross and I suspect the birds were stoking up after a forced fast. There comes a time in a quail's brief life when the food is short and the weather foul and that's when reserve body fat is all that is between the little bird and starvation.

We reached the bottom of the gully where there was a large bulldozed brush pile. Brush piles are a magnet for wildlife. I've jumped rabbits, quail, pheasants, deer, and turkeys from brush piles. A friend burns his brush piles and tells me what an ardent conservationist he is.

Dacques went on point in typical fashion, head up as if he were listening for the faint scurry of tiny quail feet. I moved toward him and Andy took the opposite side of the brush pile. A turkey sprang into the air. Dacques was demonstrating why the Brittany is called a "versatile breed." In his life, he has caught and killed a raccoon, a possum, and once, out of season, a turkey poult. So I figured he was indicating the presence of a Pilgrim centerpiece.

I opened my mouth to remonstrate in tones that would have tipped over a bulldozer . . . and a second turkey flushed, about ten feet from the dog. Dacques did not flinch. "They're gone, Dacques," I explained. "Quit fooling around."

He did not move. Dacques is a French Brittany. His name is pronounced "Doc" in Ozarkese. Down in Louisiana the French Cajuns call their dogs Phideaux: "Fido" to Yankees.

This day Dacques was not interested in coons or possums or even turkeys. He didn't even glance at the big birds as they laboriously got airborne all around him. Then a third turkey flushed almost under his nose. This was the ultimate distraction. No bird dog could resist such an intrusion on its concentration.

But Dacques did not move. I took one step and a glory of quail burst into the air. There were two bunches, each of a dozen birds. Some went toward Andy; some came back over my head. The air was filled with Missouri's favorite game bird. Dacques now broke, not being steady to wing and shot. He'd done his job; now it was time for me to do mine.

A scatter sailed over my head and I turned awkwardly, following it across the golden dead vegetation of the CRP field. The gun muzzle caught and passed it and I squeezed the trigger. The bird feathered and tumbled into the grass.

There were other birds that perfect day. I shot another along the edge of the field and headed toward the truck with six birds—two short of a limit but several more than I usually get.

It wasn't six birds that made it a perfect day; it was seeing our dog do something extraordinary. It was swinging on a bird and knowing that everything was right, that I didn't stop my swing or shoot behind. It was like launching a three-pointer in basketball and knowing as it left your hand that it was going in.

Maybe it was like going back in time and beating Andy and the neighbor kid one-on-two and feeling afterward that time is suspended and I will live forever. I was tired, but not exhausted. I could have gone on, but there was enough to the day.

The truck was up the hill and we moved toward it in what *National Geographic* photographers call the magic hour, that last hour of daylight when everything is golden. Halfway to the truck, a quail flushed and I dropped it with a snap shot that looked as if I knew what I were doing.

How can you call one bird short of a limit a perfect day? I looked at the dogs, my son, the brushy cover, the lowering day, a distant hawk circling, the silence of the evening . . .

No problem.

And I remember days that were not so perfect, that to be honest I wish hadn't happened. Once cows licked my Suburban while the dogs and I were in a grouse covert, covering it with a slime of bovine saliva.

I don't know why they licked it, but they did. Cows are not rational animals and I really don't like them. I have had bad experiences with cows. I regard cows the way political refugees regard border guards armed with Kalashnikovs. The common cow can turn a bird hunt into a nightmare of pursuit and degradation.

When I was eight, I tried to milk a cow. First she stepped on me, then she kicked the milk bucket over, then she kicked *me* over. It established the ground rules between me and cows.

I like cows best separated into their component parts and grilled over charcoal and hickory chips.

Contact between me and cows probably would have been minimal had I not become a game bird hunter. Cows and bird hunters don't mix. First, there is the red clothing which, if legend is right, turns Bossie into a rodeo Brahma, walleyed with rage. Second, bird hunters are accompanied by dogs. I'm convinced the common bovine possesses a runaway gene that makes Lillybelle imitate a murderous African water buffalo at the sight of a bird dog.

My bird dog.

Lassie may be brave enough to save drowning maidens and smart enough to have bought IBM when it was $25 a share, but I'll guarantee you that if an enraged cow comes after Lassie, that superbitch is gonna do what every dog in history has done—run to her master for help, thus attracting the cow's attention to the man behind the dog.

The kindest-looking milk cow, the one on the Borden's label representing Elsie, that lovable old milk machine, will come at you, her bag banging her hocks like the clapper of a bell tolling a death knell. She wants to stomp you and your rotten dog to rags. Possibly it's because in every cow there is the genetic memory of a wolf hanging on to its nostrils while another gnaws at its Achilles tendon.

My Brittany represents the ancestral pack. All we want is to get to the other side of the pasture, where there is an alder swamp with woodcock and a few grouse. Naught stands between us and those birds save two hundred yards of bare ground and a surly knot of cows, glaring in our direction and muttering.

It's impossible to go around because of bogs that come right to the fence line. If we try to sidle along the fence and the cows charge, we'll rip those new brush pants six ways from Sunday. If we opt to gut it out and angle warily across the pasture, Flossie and her compadres will wait for us to reach the exact geometric center of that pasture before they make their move.

A good bird dog is oblivious to cows. You could stampede the cattle holdings of the King Ranch past Ol' Streak when he's tracking a running bird and he wouldn't raise his head. That's how he gets into the middle of enemy territory before he realizes the trouble he's in. But once he notices that he is surrounded by large animals, he panics and runs for daddy, pursued by roaring creatures with large hooves and wicked horns.

Cows are prone to mob mentality. If they don't stampede toward you, they stampede over the hill away from you, past the startled herdsman who then comes looking for whoever is molesting his livestock. "But I didn't do anything!" you protest to the red-faced landowner. "I was just standing there!"

"I knew I never shoulda given you permission to hunt!" he cries. "It's that damn dog!" He stabs an accusing finger at Sal, the pointer you wouldn't take $2,000 for, and she tucks her tail between her legs and looks as guilty as a junkyard rat. The cows, meanwhile, have come to a halt fifty yards away and stand with half-hidden smirks.

Cow attacks can be either frightening or degrading. If a 2,000-pound bull gets you down on rocky ground, he's going to do bodily damage to you. But if a cow butts you spraddling through a stack of manure, the damage is emotional.

Two friends stopped at a farmhouse to ask permission to hunt. One had a large Labrador that leaped from the car and gleefully assaulted the farmer's chickens. Don plunged after his rampant Lab, wrestled him to earth (well, earth is not quite the word, since it was a barnyard), and they rolled around a bit. The commotion attracted the attention of the farmer's cows, which proceeded to wool the two unmercifully, butting them back and forth, like seals playing with a soccer ball.

The other friend, ever helpful, did the only thing possible. He leaned against the car and laughed until he nearly wet his pants.

"I hate cows," says a hunting buddy. "I absolutely hate them." Perhaps that is because he must cross the pasture of No. 13. She leads a herd that seeks to catch grouse hunters in the open and destroy them. He has fled from her more than once.

Her ear tag number is prophetic, for she once got the farmer's son down in a manure pile and mauled him, rolling him over and over. "You shoulda seen him," guffawed the farmer. "Only thing white on him was his eyeballs!"

Cows are menacing in themselves, but they also are equipped with a secondary booby trap. It is well-known to anyone who has owned a bird dog for more than five minutes that nothing in the dog's life is more refreshing than a cow-pie break. Who has not watched in stunned disbelief as his noble dog lowers its shoulder and slides gracefully through the juicy and copious leftovers of the last cow to pass by?

This may be a high point in the dog's day, but it is a low one for the owner, who suddenly remembers that he left his Porta-Pet kennel at home, so Ginger must now ride in the seat where Grandma usually rides to church.

I don't want to dwell on cow manure, for it is not the stuff of essays on anything other than politics; but not only does Ol' Streak anoint himself with eau de hockey, he also regards cow pies as you and I regard apple pies and then he wants to breathe on you and lick your ear.

I thought about cows and their interaction with hunters late one afternoon in Minnesota as we trudged wearily out of Uncle Willie's covert. Uncle Willie had separated his heifers from his bull calves. The boys had broken out and now were looking for a way into the girls' dorm. The heifers were leaning against their fence, giggling and batting their long lashes at the boys across the road.

Uncle Willie had shared his land with us and we now had to give our labor in return. No matter that we were exhausted from a seven-hour grouse hunt through boggy, tangled country, leg weary, sore of foot and sinew, hungry, chilled, wanting only rest. We had to return those cows to their pasture.

Tiredly, we ran up and down the road, waving our hands and shouting hoarsely at the horny bull calves. In that moment I gained great sympathy for high school principals who deal with hormone-scourged teenagers daily.

I brood on cows sometimes until I remember the story of Frank and Walt Olsen. Frank and Walt are Minnesota Norwegian bachelor farmers. They had a prime herd of dairy cows and routinely got up about 5:30 a.m., winter and summer, to tend to them. Frank would go to the barn to ready the milking machinery and Walt would round up the herd in a nearby pasture and bring them to the barn.

A summer storm had passed in the night. The brothers rose wordlessly, having lived together so long they communicated without speaking. Frank went to the barn, Walt to the pasture.

Walt was back uncommonly quickly, without cows. Frank looked at his brother. Walt, a man of economical speech, said simply, "Well, you don't need to hook up the machines, Frank. De're all dead."

Lightning had struck down the entire herd, a tragedy for the cows but, as it turned out, a bonanza for the brothers. The two brothers made a small fortune on insurance and selling the meat from their defunct herd and have lived happily ever after. Much as I have after learning that a higher power can intervene when cows become too pushy.

Even though the magic days will endure in my memory, the more mundane moments will not. That is why I keep a hunter's diary. The pages are scribbled and in some cases blotted and scratched. It would draw a resounding F in any elementary English class from the fifth grade up.

But it is a book of love, a book of travel, of adventure, of joy and sadness. Every hunter should have one and I'm sorry it took me thirty years to figure that out.

Actually, a diary isn't much good until the memories of the days afield have faded. Then you pick through the stained pages and those crabbed entries revive the old friends and old dogs of memory.

You think you'll never forget that day when you couldn't miss, when you doubled down by the river and the dog work was sensational. You entered it all in the diary that night, wriggling your stocking feet at the fire. You drew a little map with the covey locations marked.

And now, years later, you just came in from one of the worst hunting days you've ever had. You couldn't have hit a quail had it been perched on the bead of the gun barrel, peeking over the edge to see what was inside.

Your dog busted every covey as if his nose were made of chert while your buddy's dog performed like a Grand National finalist, a point that your buddy made in tones that sounded remarkably like a rooster at dawn.

Then your dog relieved himself on your buddy's shell vest and you had a flat tire at day's end. And something under the hood was making growling noises, as if a rusty, dying lion were trapped in there.

Sighing, you look back in your diary before you make your tear-stained entry for this rotten day, and you stumble on the best-day entry of so long ago; immediately those silver memories flood back and you feel better about things. Not perfect, understand . . . but better.

It's best to make an entry every day, in and out of hunting season, so you can record the progress of pups, your scores at skeet or trap, or maybe just the weather. You can opine in the spring about the effects of the weather on nesting birds, or later in the summer how drought and heat is affecting the hatch.

All this and more is possible with a diary. It is a record of your life afield, a chronicle of the tiny triumphs and disappointments that, strung together like a set of pearls, make a matchless necklace.

There is a discipline in sitting down with the book and a pencil each evening (sometimes I write with pen, which accounts for the blots and scratchings). You think about the day before letting it go. You don't just call it quits and sack out. What has the day held?

Why wasn't the old bridge covey there? Could it be because the landowner dozed out the brush corner and fall-plowed the soybean crop? Maybe that idea didn't occur to you when the dogs ran out of cover a half mile from where you once found birds.

Now, by the fire with the dog twitching beside you, there's time to think. There are no more covey locations to find, no growling midday gut to soothe with slimy hamburgers that would have to improve to be called garbage.

Now you've had time to think and relax; now is the time to put your thoughts and experiences on paper. No need to be creative. No need to use your diary to vent your frustrations and anger. Just put it down the way it happened and if there are problems, figure out where the blame belongs. If you've fussed at your hunting buddies, look at the conflict from both sides—chances are it was everyone's fault.

If you couldn't hit the ground with a load of no. 8 shot and blamed it all on the dog, now is the time to give him a hug and an extra dog biscuit and confess to Dear Diary.

Do you have theories on why there aren't as many quail as you thought there should be? Put them down on paper and then analyze them. Maybe they're as half-baked as most lay theories are. If so, they'll probably look dumb and save you the embarrassment of putting your foot in it with a professional.

Not that you, as a member of the consuming public, don't have a say-so in the management of quail or any wildlife. You should bellow, and loudly, when things don't go the way you want them to. You may be right. The best way to bellow is through a conservation organization—Quail Unlimited, the Ruffed Grouse Society, Pheasants

Forever, or Ducks Unlimited—there are many, all equally deserving of your support. Choose the ones you believe in the most and support them with your money and your time.

My diary—I talk about it as if I were a blushing schoolgirl confiding my most intimate secrets to it. There really are no secrets. There are a couple of entries that I'd rather people didn't know about because they are painful.

But it's generally pretty drab stuff, except to me. If you're looking for titillation, check out the adult book store—not my diary. Quail hunting seldom is grist for sensational material.

Here's a bit from a 1984 entry:

> Good day. Found two coveys north area, two in south. I missed a tough jump shot in horseweeds. Missed a meatball twice over Ginger point, finally made a nice shot on a single flush in the woods. Andy missed one easy bird twice, a tough shot once. Got into an endless field of standing corn and cockleburs way over our heads. Worst mess I ever saw. Spent half hour at car picking burs and listening to Willie Nelson. Saw two deer. Walked a long way but the exercise felt good and despite toothache, I feel better than I have for a while.

I put down my impressions *at the time* and it was a good day to me then, despite having missed some easy shots, having gotten only one quail for many miles of walking, having gotten into that awful bur field.

So what—I shared a minor adventure with good friends. We were companions in mild misery, and at the time it bonded us closer together. This might have been

forgotten had I not put it on paper. I might have remembered only the fierce burs or my awful shooting. And that
would have turned something fine into something trivial.

Here's another entry that has special meaning:

Training session for Pepper. Andy got his new gun—I
put it in car, in case, and he didn't know until he
opened the case at H.C. Enormous grin. Pepper flash-
pointed small covey or covey remnant. Don't think she
ran them up. Couldn't find them. Then Ginger and
Guff double-pointed slough covey. Brought Pepper in,
shaking like a leaf. Up they went and Andy didn't fire.
Ginger pointed a single and Andy missed his first shot
with the new double. I missed a snap shot at another
single. Never could find the bulk of the covey. Pepper
hunted very well and was enormously excited by it all.
She's a dandy. Andy is lucky.

It means nothing to you—but to me it is priceless, a
treasured memory from the family scrapbook. For Pepper
was my son Andy's first bird dog, a lovely little French
Brittany. And Andy's Christmas present, which he was
given a month early to take advantage of the quail season,
was a new double-barreled shotgun.

Andy and Pepper and I hunted many more seasons, but
it will be tough ever to top that wonderful moment on a
gray day at H.C. (I even keep the names of my honey
holes secret from myself.)

My hunter's diary is a special record of my uncommonly common life in the field and it warms my heart
and my mind beside the fire after the season is closed

and the sleet scratches with skeletal fingers at the frosted windowpane.

My diary is as much a part of the hunt as the dog and the gun. It is my scuffed, scribbled friend, and I would never again be without it. The scrawled words, sometimes almost indecipherable, stir old ashes and disclose the fire beneath. And I am warmed.

THREE

Knee Deep in Brittanies

The recipient of the Dear Pup letter I wrote (chapter 1) was McGuffin du Calembour, who was a constant companion and friend for a dozen years and the patriarch of our present kennel.

I've had Brittanies of one national origin or another for twenty years. They are my friends, more so than some humans I have known who professed to be friends but did me wrong. No Brittany ever has acted in malice toward me. Sometimes they develop a selective hearing that prevents them from hearing a shouted command at a distance of three feet, but they can hear a plate being scraped a mile away.

Sometimes they do things that they know I disapprove of—I have explained that ripe cow manure is not what I prefer as their *essence du jour*—but never have they lied to me or treated me with contempt or damaged me behind

my back. It is not in a dog to be mean-spirited; it is in the
nature of man to be, however, and good friends need to
overcome that failing.

Never will I be without my dogs unless they cart me
off to some old folks' residence that doesn't allow pets.
"They" will have to be a powerful bunch of keepers to
get that done.

Meanwhile, I enjoy the dogs and sometimes they enjoy
me. Sometimes, when I am in a rage at life and prone to
take it out on them, they tiptoe on a carpet of eggs. Most
of the time, however, they sprawl all over the room, soak-
ing up heat from the fire, bur-tangled fuzz balls twitching
from phantom hunts.

Each twitch shakes loose a few beggar's ticks, the flat
seeds of beggarweed with the Velcro surface. It's superb
quail food, but if you deposit the sticky seeds on your host-
ess's Chippendale, you'll be every bit as welcome with her
as facial blemishes on Miss America.

Fortunately, nothing in our house is Chippendale,
just chipped, so the dogs come in for a visit before they
get jailed in the kennel each night, and they drowse
by the fire. This used to send the cat into hiding with
ever-worsening psychological damage. She lived to be
nearly twenty, frightened all the way. Must have been
a terrible life.

The Vance Brittanies have had an international flavor.
Ginger was an American Brittany, while McGuffin and his
spawn are the product of illustrious French Brittany lines.

The Brittany is named for the French province of the
same name. I've never had any bird dog but a Brittany, if

you discount a setter named Pat, accepted by my father as payment on a slow debt. My father thought he was getting a bargain, but he was wrong.

I'm unashamedly in love with Brittanies. A friend says he can't quite trust anything with a red nose, which means I guess that he and Santa Claus aren't getting along, but the red nose is found only on the American Brittanies—my French dogs have cute little black noses, and my son's French Brit, Pepper, was as black all over as a Labrador retriever.

She'd be drummed out of the American Kennel Club if she were an American Brit, but such color variations not only are encouraged among the French dogs but actually bring a premium price. Out of Pepper's birth litter of eight, three were the familiar orange-and-white, three were tri-colored (brown, black, and orange), Pepper was black, and the other was a strange liver-and-yellow color.

Pepper has thrown a variety of orange-and-white and black-and-white pups. Tess, who probably carried the recessive black gene, had two litters, including one with a black-and-white boyfriend, yet all her pups were orange-and-white.

The summary of the French breed standard could have been written by someone looking at Guff: "Thickset and strong-backed. An elegant little dog, very vigorous in its movements, energetic, with an intelligent look, presenting the appearance of a full-blooded dog."

Of course, that judge needed to see Guff in the field and not sprawled on his back in front of the television, with all the grace of a walrus taking the sun. Then he looked about as full-blooded as Billy Joe Bob watching the Daytona 500 on a battered television set with a long-necked beer in his hand.

Ginger was perhaps a better bird dog, but Guff was unparalleled when it came to aggressive desire. His daughter, Pepper, is even more determined. If guts and wish could make it so, they'd have won the Grand National, one-two.

There is a World Wide Web page devoted to the French Brittany in the United States: http://www.french-Brittany.org and also one for Canada: http://132.204.160.212/~dcampbel/ceb/cebeng.htm. There you'll find the standards for the breed and by those standards a couple of our present kennel might pass the first round.

Flick has floppy lips, a fault, while Dacques and Pepper have "big and frizzy" ears. The French Brittany is supposed to fit in a square (assuming you could get one to stand still long enough). It should be as tall as it is long.

Flick is a long dog. He runs like a fire engine with someone steering the back end independently from the front, but he covers an ungodly amount of ground. Tess's three pups, which are five months old as I write this, are long-legged like their daddy Flick and perhaps will be long-bodied as well. Some might fail the prettiness standard but pass the hunting test. That, to me, is more important.

You may ask, Is there really such a thing as a French Brittany? That's a valid question. If you want to be picky, *all* Brittanies are French. The breed originated in France, and in the eyes of the several registration bodies in the United States, there is no difference between the French Brittany and the American Brittany.

However, the classified pages in *Gun Dog* magazine are specific to "Brittany" and "French Brittany," so there must be a distinction in the minds of breeders and buyers. French Brittany owners and breeders are quick to point out physical differences between French and American Brittanies, using the analogy that the two are as distinct as English and Irish setters, which are registered separately.

Even though all Brittanies obviously are French in origin, American breeders, with typical Yankee resistance to owing anybody anything, have bred a different dog over the past few decades, primarily by line breeding and cross-breeding within the country.

R. C. Busteed, a geneticist from Texas, bred brothers and sisters to get what he considered the genetically correct Brittany, an orange-and-white dog. Along with others, including Maxwell Riddle, author of *The Complete French Brittany* (Howell Books, 1974), Busteed considered black an unacceptable Brittany color. "As Dr. Busteed has pointed out," Riddle writes, "any Brittany in America which shows up with black is a mongrel. Should this happen, the situation should be reported to the American Kennel Club, and an investigation made so that the dog's registration papers can be destroyed."

With that kind of intransigence, understanding between French and American Brittany purists would be tough. But the nation's gun dog owners probably will do what the elitists won't.

Gun Dog classified ads increasingly list black-and-white French Brittanies, and if my inquiries about puppies are an indication, hunters prefer the black-and-white puppies over orange-and-white. One ad in a Kansas City newspaper read: "BRITTANY Puppies, 8 wks, AKC reg. shots, wormed, mthr French B&W, fthr o&w. If b&w $150, 3f, 2m, o&w b/blk noses $100."

I interpreted that to mean that the black-and-white dogs list for a higher price, a thumb of the nose at the American Brittany Club and its incomprehensible prejudice against black. Once a prospective puppy buyer asked me if it was true, as he had heard, that the black-and-white Brits had better noses than their orange-and-white counterparts. I'm the type who, given a job as a used car salesman, would last about one hour because I'd tell the first customer that the vintage car he was considering would be lucky to make it out of the lot. So I told the eager puppy buyer that coat color doesn't have a whole lot to do with nasal acuity. Dumb, dumb, dumb!

Casual breeders continue to mix the two Brittany breeds and unless the registering bodies soon require separate registration, a time will come when there really is only the Brittany, not French or American. It won't be the orange-and-white of the American purists nor the elegant and often multihued French dog, but it still will be a Brittany.

American Brittany breeders have expanded the breed's hunting horizons, breeding for range, so today's American Brit field trialer can run with pointers. Increasingly, though, those who hunt, especially grouse, woodcock, and quail in much of their range, are looking for closer-working dogs.

Enter the French Brit, whose field trials are walking affairs in which the rules demand a close-working dog. Many

of my puppy callers have been very specific about not
wanting "one of those damn big-running field trialers." Of
course, for every one of those callers, there might be a
dozen others who would pay big money for one of those
damn big runners.

If you're inclined to be picky, lobby to drop "spaniel"
from the dog's name. The Brittany is no more a spaniel
today than the setter is. All upland dogs have evolved
from spaniels, and pointers and setters probably have as
much spaniel in their background as Brittanies do.

Further, the Brittany is distinguished from its look-alike
spaniel cousins by the fact that it points birds instead of
flushing them. When the American Brittany Club was
formed in 1942, there was considerable discussion over
whether "spaniel" should be part of the name. An older
group, which became largely inactive during World War
II, was called the Brittany Spaniel Club of North America.
The two merged and excised "spaniel" from the club
name. The French, however, continue to use "spaniel"
(*epagneul*) as part of the breed name.

The history of the Brittany, as with every other
pointing dog, dates to the spaniels of thirteenth-century
Spain. But, as with every other pointing breed, that dog
has been changed by crossbreeding with other dogs so
many times that today's Brittany is a long way from the
historic Spanish spaniel.

In the French magazine *L'Epagneul Breton*, the official
publication of the French Club de l'Espaneul Breton,
Brit fancier Henri-Xavier Guelou speculated on the ori-
gins of the French Brits. He traced a fairly distinct fore-

bear at least to the 1600s. "Rembrandt, Jean de Steen, etc. showed a fairly small white-and-maroon (liver) spaniel with a short tail called the Breton spaniel. So, it's accepted that this dog was well-established in Europe at that time."

But dogs were used in hunting at least three hundred years before that. "Eispainolz," the Spanish spaniels, were established in the Ysel area of France and trained to hold game birds until a hunter could throw a net over them (none of this nonsense about wing shooting—since guns didn't exist that could do it anyway).

Guelou says the French Brits developed at the center of Brittany, on the Cotes-du-nord, Finistere, Morbihan, and Ille-et-Vilaine. Brittany is the part of France that juts out into the North Atlantic between the English Channel and the Bay of Biscay. It's a rough, rocky land where life was tough when the Brittany was being created.

Jeff Griffen in his *Hunting Dogs of America* perfectly sums up the Brittany in general. The French peasant

> specifically wanted a hunter that would find all types of small game to fill the pot—rabbits along the hedgerows, woodcock and duck in the marshes and beside the creeks which laced through Brittany, partridge and pheasant in the grain fields. He had to have a dog that was close-working and ever obedient, because the vast majority of his hunting was poaching.

There! It's out! The Brittany is an outlaw's dog and the next time yours chases a rabbit, don't yell at him. He's just obeying several centuries of judicious breeding.

The description of the ideal Brittany is "cob," which denotes a stocky animal that is hell-for-stout. Welsh cobs are horses developed to work in mines. They are called the strongest horses for their size in the world. A year after the first French Brittany breed standards were drawn up in 1907, the word "cob" became the summary description of the ideal dog.

Most early French Brits apparently were either liver-and-white or black-and-white. Interestingly, French breeders thought black-and-white indicated English forebears and with typical French Anglophobia denied registration to the color from 1910 to 1956 (they also barred long-tailed puppies between 1910 and 1933—puppies had to be naturally short-tailed).

Today, the black-and-white and tricolor patterns are acceptable in France. In the United States, black-and-white French Brits are in demand because they're unusual, even though the American Kennel Club won't allow them to be bench-shown.

The English influence in the development of French Brittanies is typical of the strange dog attitude between the two countries. An article in *L'Epagneul Breton* by Andre Garnier said it this way: "Around 1865, English lords came over to Brittany to hunt woodcock and partridge. They brought their dogs with them, mainly setters, pointers and even springers. As Great Britain already had a quarantine law, our English friends left their 'companions' behind on farms."

According to the prevailing view, at least in France, these English orphans (and some later deliberate crosses) bred with the native dogs of Brittany, the poachers' dogs, to produce a somewhat larger hunting animal that is today's French Brittany—an amalgam of setter, pointer, perhaps springer, and Duke's-mixture native dog. By 1896, there were several "variable spaniels" shown at the Paris Exposition, including one black-and-white dog and another chestnut-and-white.

It was at this point that breeders began to think seriously about developing a distinct breed, with size and color standards. The first breed club formed in 1907. Remember—there were other spaniel clubs in France at the time, just as there are other spaniel clubs today. The Brittany was a hat-in-hand relative with dubious lineage asking to be recognized. It was as if you or I applied to be royalty because Cousin Charlie claimed to be descended from the Romanovs.

Even into the 1920s, yesterday by evolutionary standards, the French Brittany was being tinkered with genetically. The Brittany Club of France had only forty-eight members. By 1930, there were 250 members.

As late as 1935, there were only 854 French Brittany puppies whelped in France (for practical purposes, all that were whelped anywhere). World War II interrupted the development of the dogs, which had become popular on the field trial circuit. In 1946, breeders got back into action with more than 1,600 puppies whelped. Today, there are nearly 2,000 members in the French Brittany Club and the dog is the fourth largest breed in France, with nearly 5,000 registrations annually.

Registering a French Brittany is tougher in France than it is in this country where, if you have the money, the

American Kennel Club will register the dog. Puppy registration is provisional in France. The dog must be looked at and qualified as an adult by designated examiners and dogs that don't meet the breed standards are blackballed.

Brittany field and bench trials are also tougher in France, since both field and bench dogs must have placed or won in the other discipline before they can gain a championship in their own, in other words, a show dog must also have placed in a field trial and a field trial dog must have placed in bench competition.

French field trials are walking competition, and the dog must work in a way that would disqualify almost every American hunting dog. It can hunt out a hundred meters or so to either side, but when it crosses in front of the handler, it must be within gun range, an unheard-of requirement in the United States.

Dave Follansbee, first editor of *Gun Dog*, is the Yankee guru of the French Brit, one of the first to import and breed the dogs in the United States. He tried to sum up the dog in a September-October 1982 article in *Gun Dog*. "Consistency of type, consistency of pattern, ideal range, great intensity and desire, combined with a very stable and biddale disposition, sweetness of temperament, eagerness to please, a very high order of intelligence and, of course, the black nose and dark eyes on orange and white dogs and the black and white and black tricolor dogs." Save for the color patterns, none of that would violate what any hunting dog owner wants from his dog, no matter the breed.

It probably boils down to the black nose and dark eyes, as opposed to the American Brittany's amber eyes and rose nose. Follansbee, who got me into French Brittanies with his unbridled enthusiasm, maintained that the French dogs had "more elegant heads" than their American cousins.

But *Gun Dog* readers have written me that they've seen American Brits that could be easily mistaken for French dogs if you went by conformation. And, save for their black-and-white coloration, Dacques and Chubbs, my two littermates, could be mistaken for American Brittanies. They have broad heads and muzzles and, looking at a head-and-shoulders portrait, you'd be hard-pressed to tell them from setters.

French Brit owners should start by encouraging the American Brittany Club (1392 Big Bethel Road, Hampton, Virginia 23666) to lobby for separate registration. The ABC has been setting Brittany standards for the American Kennel Club since 1942. They refuse to recognize American and French Brittanies as separate breeds and have ignored repeated requests by me to consider the idea.

The North American Versatile Hunting Dog Association (NAVHDA; Box 520, Arlington Heights, IL 60006; tel. 708-255-1120) registers and recognizes French Brittanies as a separate breed. The American Field (542 South Dearborn, Chicago, IL 60605; tel. 312-663-9797) does not make the breed distinction but would be agreeable to argument if there were a French Brittany Club to make it. It also registers foreign-registry dogs but requires considerable documentation.

In order for the French Brittany to be recognized as a separate breed by the American Kennel Club, there must be a certain number of dogs in the country, distributed geographically. The AKC first would list French Brittanies in the "miscellaneous class." Then French Brit owners would have to form a national breed club with an accurate stud book, supervised by the AKC. Then *maybe* the French Brittany would be recognized as a separate breed—after many years of waiting, hat in hand.

While the AKC will register tricolor and black-and-white Brittanies, it will not allow them to be bench shown, a peculiar prejudice. The AKC breed list is filled with inconsistencies (for example, a colored bull terrier and a white bull terrier or three-color variations for the cocker spaniel). Roger Caras, the well-known dog expert and writer/commentator, says that "there are scads of changes, but it is going to take forever to make them. In the meantime it is up to knowing and caring breeders of Brits to keep the two breeds apart and not cross them."

Bill Dillon of Wagner, South Dakota, has founded a French Brittany breed club. The e-mail address is bretonclub @usa.net and the Web page is http://www.french-Brittany. org. The mailing address is 30242 Chalk Rock Road, Wagner, South Dakota 57380.

Brittanies have picked up a bum rap as close-working dogs. I would have put Ginger in her youthful prime against any chert-headed pointer who ever slipped the leash and headed over the hill, not to be seen again until feeding time.

Once I took her to South Dakota. When I let her out of the car at the fringe of the 115,000-acre Fort Pierre National Grassland, her eyes got big and she started looking herself over to see whether she had died and gone to heaven. In the distance jackrabbits perked their ears and swallowed uneasily, for one of their peers was afoot.

There was a swooshing roar and Ginger vanished, a dusty blur headed for the horizon. Occasionally I would see a tiny speck at the ridge top, which I surmised to be either Ginger or a sprinting antelope.

Close working? Sure—like a cruise missile. I think the historic Brittanies and today's French Brit are bred for walking hunters and like to hunt to the cover and keep contact with their hunter/master. Close in thick stuff, wide-ranging in the open.

Ginger, the American Brit, was street people, a back alley bitch who was born to spend her life rummaging in a garbage can, one eye peeled for the cops. She was an American Brittany but without papers, and she went through three owners before she came to me, flaky and flighty, a year old and having no clear idea of what she was supposed to do except run.

It was hard to think of her as a street survivor when she was nuzzling my hand on a sharp winter night as we sat in front of a comfortable fire watching the flames pirouette to the hypnotic rhythms of combustion. I was listening to Mozart. I didn't know what she was listening to—probably the wild song that had always been her theme. Ginger didn't even look much like a Brit. She had poodle-cut ears like a . . . well, a poodle, maybe, or a curly-coated retriever. Her head was narrow and her eyes faintly Oriental. She belied her allegedly pure blood with her looks.

A Brittany? It was hard to believe except when she was locked on a point so solid it would take a low-yield nuclear device to get her attention. She was a canine conundrum who alternately brightened my life and made it intolerable. I cursed her and I loved her. Mostly, I think, I loved her. Ginger never was a mean dog. She was the dog you leave with the babies and toddlers, for they could fall on her and pull her stupid-looking ears without fear of retribution.

She never did calculatedly mean things. It's just that she was of the elements. She acted because of forces that came from far out in the Universe. She was a dog, motivated by primal drives. She heard commands that I didn't give. She lived to hunt and no love is greater than that, including the one she had for me.

Where the average dog is content polishing his master's shoes with the underside of his muzzle, the Out There is what Ginger wanted. There were always horizons untouched by the once lean, then middle-aged, portly bitch who troubled my life for nearly a decade and who finally found a horizon that I have yet to cross.

Yes, she loved me in her way and, yes, she wanted her petting when that was going 'round. But there was always a voice calling the old girl, somewhere outside the door, somewhere . . . out there.

Ginger was part cat, I think. Inscrutable. I never knew what was behind those nutty eyes, those amber orbs that glowed with alien life. There were thoughts in that narrow head that I've never read in any other dog. I think I know dogs pretty well, but Ginger was something else. She was like no dog of my experience.

While the interior of her nose was a computer to rival something from the IBM labs, the exterior was a shambles. It's like the riches of King Tut's located inside a beer joint outhouse. She had a calico nose, part pink, part a muddy brown. American Brits have red noses, French Brits black noses. Ginger? Maybe something out of the Bermuda Triangle. Her eyes were ditch water brown and when they had that periodic crazed fire in them, they gave her a manic expression.

Ever try to tame the wind? Ginger was the wind, a chinook melting the miles under a hot tread. There are high-velocity bullets registering fewer fps than she did in her prime. I nearly left her in Iowa and again in Minnesota. "The hell with that rotten bitch!" I fumed, starting the car each time. "If she wants to live up here, let her!" And about that time, she'd trot around the corner, tongue hanging out, the hot spark of wanderlust slowly fading. Who knows what bird treasures she'd put up somewhere over the hill. I sure didn't.

And then she killed my best friend. I blamed her for Chip's death. He was a Brittany who was smart and loyal and devoted to me. When she came in heat and I let them out of the pen, she ran for the horizon with Chip in hot pursuit. Three days later, he lay dead on the highway and I was desolate. I blamed her for trailing her irresistible lure behind her as she led poor, bemused Chip in front of a pickup truck.

I tried to give her away, but no one wanted her. So I took her back, ignored her, gritted my teeth with angry grief, and sometimes pounded on her vengefully and stupidly. She was pregnant, of course, bred by every stud mongrel within a dozen miles of my home, and so I couldn't even let her have Chip's pups and thus keep a part of him.

We spayed her.

That rotten bitch! I cursed her countless times as she left, running like an arrow from the bow. If my attention wandered for an instant, she was gone and she'd come home when it pleased her, penitent, her attitude servile. But in those hot, muddy eyes, I recognized that she was obedient to a master who was not me.

Came the next hunting season and she was the elder dog now. I had McGuffin by then, Guff, who helped fill the aching void left by Chip's death. Guff pointed and re-trieved his first quail at less than six months. But Ginger had the experience. Still, she roamed out of sight and out of hearing, doing God knows what, but now not as often. Perhaps the vet's knife had cut some of the wildness out of her, along with her swollen ovaries.

She never slowed, never faltered. She flowed through the brush like a spirit, and by season's end she was painfully thin, a bag-of-bones bitch who'd worn herself down to skin and guts. Other dogs lay in the kennel, banged up with pad tears or swollen knees or bloody wounds. Not Ginger. Nothing but sinew and dandruffy hair.

Still ready to go.

I shot grouse and pheasants and woodcock and quail over her that year and began to realize that she was some-thing I'd never known before—a true bird dog. She wasn't a pet. She lived to hunt, not to be pampered.

Finally, I realized she was motivated by forces that were more elemental than anything I'd ever known. She responded to the stars, the moon, the tides, and the seasons. She couldn't help it. She was a creature of the earth, not subject to the constrictions that rule us.

Of all the bird dogs I've owned or been around, Ginger was the only one who truly was mesmerized by bird scent. I saw her, at the flush, come back to awareness as if her mind had been far away. Her glazed eyes slowly cleared and became alert, and she visibly sorted out her wits.

There never was a worry about her breaking a point. She couldn't if she had tried. She was muscle locked. If ever there was a role model for the apocryphal story about the lost dog who pointed so intently it starved to death, Ginger was it.

Ginger had a good nose, not a fifty-yarder, but somehow at day's end, her box score showed her among the leaders. She was a stylish pointer, head down, leaning into the point with nothing moving. There was no doubt. She was like some models, plain in person and really not symmetrical . . . but she photographed well. You could shove a bird in her mouth and she'd hold it as gently as if it were made of bone china, and do it all day.

Even into her declining years she still occasionally took off when my back was turned. And when she was gone I knew that she wouldn't be back until the fire burned out of her.

What I feared each time was that she would get herself killed, like Chip. All her Houdini escape skills wouldn't mean a thing if some jerk in a car smashed the hot life out of her. But she always showed up, usually in the morning. On one occasion she wasn't back by bedtime, nor when I got up at 2 a.m. There was rolling thunder in the distance and lightning lit the empty street. I fell asleep uneasily. It stormed and I came half-awake, wondering if Ginger were huddled miserably somewhere in the hissing rain. But I figured she hadn't gotten this far in life without adapting to unpleasant conditions.

I was up early and she was at the door, wet, muddy and as penitent as she always was, the predatory fire gone from her eyes. She was like an alcoholic. I fixed a tasteless breakfast, made even more so because of a severe head cold, and was moodily shoveling it in when I felt a gentle pressure on my knee. I looked down. Ginger nestled her head there, asking forgiveness. And what could I do? I gave it to her.

She didn't die in the Out There; she died at the vet's, a victim of poisoning. I don't know, but I suspect she ate tainted meat from a deer one of my neighbors had dressed and pitched in the ditch down the hill from his house. It was an ignominious end for the old girl. Ginger became a memory of sunshine and rain, like life itself, the dog whose ultimate allegiance was to her gypsy genetics.

We did not place a headstone on her grave. She lies in the dog equivalent of Potter's Field, the location forgotten but not the dog. Her epitaph is not on a marker, but on my heart and in my mind. It reads: "Well, boys, she had a good run."

I'm guessing the Brittany is the sporting breed growing fastest in popularity. It was only about thirty years ago that I started hearing about Brittanies, though they've been around for many years. When I made the decision to have my own bird dogs, I went with what, at that time, was an unfamiliar breed. Why a Brittany? Because it is a natural pointer with a strong retrieving instinct, loves to hunt dead . . . and simply cannot be spoiled as a hunting dog by giving it hugs and kisses.

Brittanies are among the most affectionate dogs on earth, consummate ear lickers who can adore you with their eyes until you get embarrassed. Try hugging the average rock-ribbed pointer and you'll be lucky if you don't get stone bruises. Setters, German shorthairs, even Drathaars, all have drawbacks as companions in a hugging contest, but the Brittany invites snuggling even when wet and full of burs.

On the other hand, maybe there's something to be said for dogs who function efficiently and don't invite love. It's less of a heart tug the day you lose them.

While Brittanies are fairly new on the American hunting scene, let me point out to pointer dogmatics (sorry about that) that spaniels were graciously including their masters in hunting exploits long before the first pointer or setter came loping down the lane with a badly chewed game bird halfway down its throat.

Way back in 1686, Nicholas Cox wrote in *The Gentleman's Recreation*

It is now the mode to shoot flying, as being by experience found the best and surest way, for when your game
is on the wing it is more exposed to danger; for if but
one shot hits any part of its wings so expanded, it will
occasion its fall, although not to kill it, so that your
spaniel will soon be its victor.

Cox never saw me shoot or he wouldn't have put in that
part about the surest shot being a wing shot, but he was
talkin' spaniel before there was such a thing as a pointer
or setter.

In 1517, Dr. Johannes Caius, University of Cambridge,
said, "When he (the bird dog) hath found the bird, he
keepeth a sure and fast silence and stayeth his steps and
will proceed no further and with close covered, watching
eye layeth his belly to the ground and so creepeth forward
like a worm."

I remember a crisp day when Guff halted at a weed
patch and stayethed his steps. Then, with watching eye,
he layethed his belly to the ground and so creepethed forward like a worm. I call it "walking on eggs." It says, "Boss,
I know there are birds close-by and I'm gonna tiptoe until
I find them for you."

It was a pretty sight to see him sleuthing carefully, a
few inches at a time, until he froze on point, his mouth
whuffing as if he had run into a stultifying fantasy of stink,
a numbing fog of bird smell.

Brittanies adjust instantly to the good life. Bring the
average bird dog inside after life in a kennel and it is wary,
like a Skid Row bum brought in from the alley and offered

Chateau Lafitte '34, a Cuban cigar, and a T-bone steak. The Brittany would accept such hospitality as his due and perhaps bark demandingly for seconds.

Okay, I suppose I have to admit that the Brittany is not perfect. Sir Isaac Newton's spaniel knocked over a lamp and burned his priceless manuscripts. It's a wonder apples don't fall up today. My dogs have, shall we delicately say, defiled a manuscript or two, carelessly left within range, and I suppose this is critical comment, but I'd rather not think about it.

Brittanies tend to be generalists as hunters, able to hunt all birds pretty well, but probably not superlatively on any of them. I have hunted bobwhite and scaled quail, ruffed and sharp-tailed grouse, pheasants, prairie chickens, woodcock, snipe, and doves with my Brittanies and they don't even pause to shift gears. They have a Hydramatic Hunting transmission and slip seamlessly from one bird to another.

They also are avid squirrel and rabbit hunters. Dacques now has a life list that includes a raccoon, an opossum, and a wild turkey poult.

I now must confess that the modern Brittany is a created dog, a refinement of raw materials so crude that the average junkyard dog, given a few generations of selective breeding, could become a passable Brit.

Dave Follansbee, who once raised French Brittanies in a Fifth Avenue apartment, is the guru of the Gallic Brits in this country and he wrote thus of them in *Gun Dog* magazine: "Until 1906, the Brittany was hardly more than a mongrel, because the native Breton dog, itself only vaguely defined as a type, had been crossed with a dozen or more English and continental pointing breeds, not to mention a few flushing breeds."

A bit later, oh, horror of horrors! he confesses, "What that first French standard could not remedy, however, was the realization that the first Brittanies constituted an incredibly *impure* breed."

But what has evolved over the past century is an incredibly cute dog, who also is a fine little hunter with the guts of an NFL running back. Guff couldn't run through brick walls after birds . . . but he would try. Pepper once was nearly fileted by a barbed-wire fence and she didn't even yip. She came home with a flap of hide the size of Rhode Island hanging loose, wanting to play, after a full day's hunt.

You may claim that such courage is actually a lack of good sense. Any pointer will attempt the impossible dream and suffer as a result. Setters spend most of the season with bloody appendages—tails, ears, and so on.

But Brittanies aren't too dumb to know better. They just like to hunt. I know. I asked them. Brittany intelligence is legendary. It takes a mighty smart dog to find a cow pie to roll in where there haven't been cows for years. You may call this luck or a good nose, but I call it creative degradation.

I could tell you stories about Brittanies that would curl your hair, not to mention the delicate sensibilities of postal inspectors. I recall some backseat shenanigans by my dog Chip and a delicate setter named Samantha that made Fanny Hill look like a nursery rhyme.

"Now the dogs which are to be made for this pleasure should be the most principal, best and lustiest spannyels you can get, both of good scent and good courage, yet young and as little as may be acquainted with hunting," said Richard Surflet in 1600.

Chip was one of the lustiest spannyels I've ever known and it was that tendency which cost him his life when he left home in pursuit of Ginger, who was wanton (not to mention "wanting") and, eyes on the promised land, he swaggered in front of a car and found a different promised land.

I've kenneled my dogs on trips in the past few years rather than let them free range in the vehicle. No Brittany takes kindly to imprisonment. They are not a dog to crouch in a dog box wondering what's going on outside. No, the Brittany is an assistant driver without whom the driver (me) is likely to run off in roadside fields and decorate trees. Doesn't matter which Brittany—they all have the same intense curiosity about the world that surrounds them.

My Brittany is a friend and associate in hunting, a warm shoulder and a sympathetic (and soft) ear when I have the blues. He or she never judges nor criticizes and accepts my many faults without second thought. My Brittany is family.

He is my friend for too short a time and when he is gone, there will be an unending ache that time can dull but not erase.

He is here with his head on my knee, checking to make sure I say it right and don't misspell his name. But even if I did, he would shrug and lick my ear and suggest we go hunting. His solutions for all life's problems are simple—go hunting, an activity that you love, above all else, with someone you love.

It may be that the Brittany has come up with the solution to personal if not world peace.

FOUR

A Dynasty of Brittanies

McGuffin du Calembour—Guff—was a warm and constant presence for the dozen years of his life. He helped me through my midlife crisis and into my old-age crisis.

We grew grizzled and gimpy together, our joints popping, our hair turning gray. But we retained our eye for the well-turned leg (his ideal had more hair on it than mine) and the ideally prepared meal (one that is available when you're hungry).

Guff and his descendants have been with me for nearly a third of my life, these French Brittanies with the Calembour surname. Before that I had American Brittanies for a decade. More than a quarter of a century's worth of Brittanies. Not "Brittany spaniels." Spaniels are flushing dogs and our dogs *point*.

They are not flushing dogs and though they owe their heritage to spaniels, so does every other bird dog. Might as well talk about English pointer spaniels or Irish setter spaniels. Long ago the American Brittany Club dropped the "spaniel" and so has the American Kennel Club. Oddly, the French continue to speak of "Brittany spaniels." And Dave Follansbee, the American godfather of the French Brittany, founder of the Calembour line, does too.

But then the French have never exactly marched to an Anglo-Saxon drumbeat.

My American Brits were corrupted by Yankee blood. All Brittanies came from France originally. They originated in the French province of Brittany.

But the first influx of Brittanies got genetically tinkered with until they became something else. They have red noses and amber eyes and they have been bred for field trials until today you need a horse to keep up with them.

Not so the French Brit, which retains a darker nose and darker eyes and which, most importantly, retains a desire to hunt with its master. If there is a general difference between the two, it is that the American Brittany hunts for itself, while the French Brittany hunts in partnership.

And I know that will bring howls of disagreement, but that's what's known as tough noogies. I know what I know—don't confuse me with facts.

You won't find a black-and-white American Brittany either. There is a foul prejudice against black as a color in the American Brit, as if it were the black soul of the dog shining through. Well, two of our current seven French Brittanies are black-and-white and I wouldn't trade them for a coal scoop of American Brittany genes, all color corrected.

I could call our bunch a "dynasty" except I understand there was once a television program with that name and with more steamy sex. Although, come to think of it, when Guff and Gypsy were shamelessly cavorting in our backyard, it was far more graphic than anything you'd ever see on network television. (At least the neighbors thought so . . .) So I eliminated "Dynasty" as a title for this book.

Inspiration is said to strike in the pit of night, only we rarely remember it come morning. I woke up in the middle of the night, the phrase "The Neoprene Idiot" in my mind. "The perfect title!" I exclaimed and drifted back into a more normal dream featuring me and a starlet, any starlet. Oddly, I remembered the title the next morning. You see how a writer's mind works (calling that "work" is like suggesting a getaway weekend at the Internal Revenue Service headquarters).

Now all I need is a story to go with it. Maybe this guy comes home six hours late and stumbles to the front door to be met by a wife who accuses, "You have Neoprene on your breath again!" But where to go from there?

My mind began to make freewheeling associations between the brand-names I know and possible stories: "The fat lady checked into the diet control center and was issued a Thinsulate gown." Or "the hombre from Cordura . . . he's tough." Or "the bullfighter was caught on the horns of a massive bull but was protected by his Gore-tex suit of lights."

One of my books is entitled *Confessions of an Outdoor Maladroit* and one of three readers asks me what "maladroit" means and the other two are too ashamed to admit they don't know. A literate editor (an obvious oxymoron) insisted on the title.

I'd heard that cookbooks and books on hunting deer always make money and steamy sex also sells, so I suggested "Cooking Your Deer for the Playmate of the Month," subtitled "Hot, Juicy Venison." But since this book is about dogs and has no deer in it, nor, dammit, playmates of the month either, I needed something that suggested dogs.

And then my dog peed on Santa Claus and I had a title . . . "Peeing on Santa Claus." After all, an author with "Vance" in his name (folklorist Vance Randolph) wrote *Pissing in the Snow*, a collection of folktales and jokes; I could write about Guff hosing Santa Claus, the genial Christmas spirit, on New Year's Eve. As a celebration of passage, it fell far short of watching a ball drop down a track in Times Square, even listening to the Dorsey Orchestra playing "Auld Lang Syne."

But it was in keeping with certain urinary traditions established by Guff. He set an example for his descendants when he saturated my leg as I chatted with admiring fans at a field trial. They thought it was funny. Guff apparently thought it was okay. I thought . . . well, let's keep this thing on a moral plane, okay. (And if I were making puns, I'd say that a moral plane is Billy Graham's personal jet.)

Apparently field trials brought out a form of competitiveness in McGuffin that expressed itself directly through his urethra. The only other time I entered him in a field trial, he also hosed me on the leg. Perhaps he didn't like field-trialing. I'm not so hot about it myself either, but I never expressed my opinions quite so graphically. Dogs would make good critics. Never mind cogent analysis, incisive dissection. If you don't like it, simply piss on it.

But this book is not about dogs making water on their owners. That's such a silly phrase: "making water." They don't make water; they make urine and it doesn't smell like water. Eliminatory allusion would seem to be a fertile, sorry, field for a title.

We once had a collie and in the many years of his life, we never once saw him hunker to relieve himself. Collies are born with a sense of modesty rare in dogs. You would not see Lassie, en route to save a baby inadvertently left on the train tracks, pause to lift his leg and pee on Timmy.

Read a few of the old Albert Payson Terhune books about Lad and Bruce and the other noble creatures of his fables, and you couldn't imagine them squatting to relieve themselves any more than you could imagine the Queen of England or Henry Kissinger.

Pepper, on the other hand, the French Brittany queen of our kennel, once forced the United Parcel Service truck to wait for five minutes while she finished her toilette in the middle of the driveway. To her and to most bird dogs, the world is a giant litter box. While bathroom humor is not usually the subject, even in passing, of a dog book, excretion has made for some unforgettable moments.

No, this book is about a dynasty of dogs; specifically French Brittanies.

There is the reality of thousands of miles on the road with Guff's nose pressed to the windshield on the passenger side as he studies bird habitat. He can read it every bit as good as I can at sixty miles per hour and perhaps he wonders why we don't stop and investigate that good-looking fencerow.

There is the reality of Guff, golden-furred amid glittering foxtail, locked on an immovable point.

There is the reality of Guff nestling his head under my armpit as I hug him and realize, with a sudden lump in my throat, that he is getting old.

And there is the heartbreaking reality of Guff dying alone at the vet's because neither of us could do anything for him.

Maybe it's appropriate to start with a new year. All things are possible, all dogs are going to have the season of their lives, all shots will be true, all . . . well, most things look bright at the beginning.

The old year ran out, not with a bang but with a series of whimpers, groans, and whines. It started raining around Christmas, drizzled all through the holiday, effectively drenching my plans to hunt quail every day. My dream of frost-covered fields bathed in cold winter sun clabbered like old milk and I sulked in the family room, watching stupid movies on television as the quail fields turned to slime under the chilling, persistent wet.

Work was a horror and I couldn't have been more reluctant to get up in the morning had I been facing the gibbet. At least with the gibbet it's all over in a few seconds, aside from a stiff neck. That awful office goes on and on.

The vet thought Ginger, the last of my American Brittanies, had had a stroke. She was getting on in years and had overextended herself on a hunt in deep snow. We both had trouble making it back to the car, but she had more trouble than me.

McGuffin, the first of my French Brittanies, bounded through the snow like a frolicking elk—no problem for him. He was in life's prime, had mated, had a daughter, and was a grandfather, all by the time he was seven years old.

Ginger, however, was glassy-eyed and obviously sick. In addition to the concern I felt for the old girl, I was also bummed out because each pill we shoved down her obviously had been plated with 24-karat gold. If the vet wasn't vacationing on the Riviera, it wasn't because he couldn't afford it.

Mr. Internal Revenue sent me a belated Christmas greeting, a respectful proposal to "adjust" my tax bill by $1,200 in their favor. Was I getting the Rockefeller mail by mistake? No, it had my name on it. I'd like to adjust his nose so he could smell his ear wax.

Marty and I had an argument that resulted in me spending New Year's Eve pouting and watching a terrible sci-fi movie while she went to bed, no doubt wondering why she hadn't married her high school sweetheart. The last grains of sand in the year's hourglass ran out after I fell asleep, and the new year came in during a dreamless night.

It being a new year, I resolved to start things anew. Marty and I made up—we always do, once I realize it's my fault. Ginger looked much better and pleaded to go and I petted her and told her "pretty soon." Mr. Revenue undoubtedly had made a mistake and soon would send me a cute card telling me so. Work was three days away, an eternity.

And a sharp cold front had booted the low, nasty clouds out ahead of it and the first day of the new year was diamond clean, glittering with hard promise. The pale winter sun washed the frost-rimed fields with cold light and the sky was an endless washed-out blue.

Ah, with what high hopes I leaped from bed and gobbled a bowl of sugar-coated horse food! A day in the quail fields when, past history notwithstanding, I would fill the air with feathers and litter the ground with the bodies of small gallinaceous game birds! (Tell me again, General Custer, what are your plans for those Indians over the hill?)

I'd just gotten a letter from my Minnesota hunting buddy, Ted Lundrigan, who had hunted with me in the very area where I now planned to go. We'd run up nine coveys, a banner day, and Ted had killed a limit that included three doubles. He tossed around phrases describing me like "master tactician" and "brilliant strategist." I felt like a Bonaparte of the boonies. Come to think of it, though, Napoleon lost the war.

No matter—new year, new day a-dawning! "Here I come, quail, ready or not!" The Brittanies bounced around and chortled, "Oh boy! Oh boy!" They have unbounded faith in their daddy, which doesn't say much for the intelligence of Brittanies. I decided to take Guff, of course, and his two grandkids, the Brittany Brothers, Dacques (Doc in translation) and Chubby.

I took my old gun from my new Christmas-present case and put on my new Christmas-present shell vest and my new Christmas-present orange cap. A new year, new duds, a new beginning.

The air temperature was slightly above freezing and although the knobby ground was hard, there was a film of greasy mud on the surface. I search in vain for a simile to describe walking conditions, but "slicker than deer guts on a doorknob" comes to mind. Every step was a mini-adventure in balance. I felt like one of the Wallenda family on an extremely bad night—and a bad night for them means some serious broken bones.

Think of walking barefoot through an acre of doorknobs. Get the picture?

The air was split by crows shouting at one another and I thought about all the epithets people lay on crows: "black bandits" and "feathered marauders." Perhaps crows are just having fun. I doubt any crow hatches thinking, "Boy, I'm gonna make Farmer Jones's life miserable when *I* grow up!" Whatever crows do, they do because they're crows.

And I was doing what I do because I'm me, I guess, plodding mile after slickery mile behind tiring Brittanies, getting ever farther from the car.

There are enough chores around our house to keep Bob Vila and his entire *This Old House* crew busy for an entire television season, but here I was, following dogs around all day for (if I am lucky) a couple of eight-ounce birds.

The area I was hunting is managed for quail, which translates to fourteen-foot-high horseweeds with stalks as big around as your wrist. By January, half of them are jack-strawed in a million directions and getting through them is no more difficult than running through the Chicago Bears defensive line. Quail that survive until January have learned that those horseweeds are wonderful places to lay up, telling survival stories and snickering as cursing hunters stumble past.

The dog brave enough to get far enough inside to find quail makes as much noise as a rhinoceros dance party with music by Kiss. Understandably, quail are alerted about five minutes before the dog is able to smell them and it's a rare covey that sits around waiting for gunfire.

The first covey of the day was a muted rumble and a microsecond glimpse of birds above the weed tops. No idea where they went, but a guessing man would figure they'd bopped to the next horseweed haven a hundred yards away. Dacques and Chubby appeared looking guilty, and I gave them the obligatory chewing out.

I had resolved to walk until I broke out of my mulligrubs. It promised to be a long day. The horizon is far off where I hunt and I worked to it, then headed east, finally made the swing back toward the car. Four hours into the hunt and I hadn't fired a shot.

Late in the afternoon, I needed to cross a small creek. The crossing itself was no problem, a simple thirty-foot-long jump across running water. But getting down to the creek was a trick. It was a steep bank (the Grand Canyon by comparison is a gentle slope). I figured I could hang on to the base of a tree at the top of the bank, lower myself to an exposed root, then to another, and sooner or later I'd be at the bottom.

It was sooner. My foot slipped off the root and I shot down the bank like a greased wombat. Not wanting to learn free-fall acrobatics the hard way, I hung grimly onto the tree and pretty soon was doing my world-famed imitation of an orangutan.

The other elbow caromed off something sharp and pain shot up the arm and right out the top of my head. My camera lens scooped a glop of mud out of the bank and the butt of my shotgun slathered loose some more. I groaned and let go. I slid down the bank like an otter, though not in the interest of play, and landed in knee-deep ice water. I waded out of the stream, clutching my elbow and my remaining dignity, and made a speech to an uninterested Brittany about agony and the tribulations of Man.

Hunkered over in pain, looking like the loser in a mud wrestling contest, I limped back to the car. The dogs were pad-sore and bur bound.

If this was the new year, give me the old one. At least I had both elbows working. I stood at the car and totaled the day: Five hours, no shots, only one real covey and a couple of rag-tag remnants. Dogs failed to make a single point and quit on me halfway back to the car. My feet hurt from slithering around on the corrugated ground.

My face was chapped and my lips split. On the other hand . . . Think of all the benefits. I had toned my muscles in Nature's gymnasium, the ones I didn't rip from their

moorings. I spent an invigorating day afield with my faithful companions (and would spend a long, bleary night
picking cockleburs out of them).

Guff stuck his head under my armpit while I worried
cockleburs from his sides. I leaned down and gently kissed
the top of his head. It meant nothing to him, I suppose,
but it meant something to me.

FIVE

A Frenzy of Teeth

The compulsion to chew is every bit as developed in the average Brittany as it is in the exceptional beaver or muskrat, save that the beaver under most conditions performs a valuable ecological service, and the muskrat does no real damage.

But a Brittany with a full set of teeth can undermine the foundations of the Chrysler Building in one hour of unattended gnawing. In other dogs, the urge to chew is deep but controllable. In the Brittany it goes right to the core. The roots of those teeth are deeper than those of a bicentennial oak.

I suspect it has to do with boredom. A Brittany is more inquisitive than a yard full of raccoons and is restless when not intellectually challenged.

But perhaps it's not just Brittanies. Start any group of dog owners talking about canine mishap and you'll uncover an adder's nest of chew stories. Like my friend who left a Labrador in his vehicle while he went duck hunting. The Lab shredded a case of shotgun shells ("do you have any *idea* how many shells there are in a case!" he exclaimed) and was working its way through the seat padding when he came back.

My hunting buddy Spence Turner refers to himself as "a rotund trout biologist." Spence is fond of snack food on the road but, ever conscious of his weight, tries to make it diet-friendly. However, his idea of diet-friendly probably wouldn't be well received in the hallowed halls of Weight Watchers. Once he headed for north Missouri to help at a deer check station.

But he decided to quail hunt en route and took along two bird dogs in a portable kennel in the back of his venerable Volvo station wagon. His good clothing, needed for the next day's work, was in a duffel bag on the passenger seat beside him, unzipped.

Between him and the bag was a sack of chocolate-covered raisins (health food with a twist). In the kennel nestled two lanky setters, each sure in its own mind that today was its day to be in the field.

Spence parked and released one setter. He confined the other, ignoring the hurt eyes, the pouting lips. This is where the inventive dog kicks in. Spence's portable kennel had a broken latch, but he solved the problem by moving it close enough to the rear hatch that it couldn't open. Or so he thought.

The dog managed to scoot the kennel backward until it had enough room to wriggle out of the kennel and up over the top into the front seat, where it proceeded to eat two pounds of chocolate-covered raisins.

This was a digestive time bomb with a short fuse.

While the dog waited for the raisins to thunder through its alimentary canal, a tsunami of shit, it began to chew the headliner out of the wagon. When the inevitable urgency arrived, the dog chose Spence's open duffel bag for its copious deposit.

Spence returned to the car a couple of hours later, took in the devastation of his vehicle and his clothing, and cried, *"He ate my chocolate-covered raisins!"* It wouldn't be so bad if dogs merely chewed up things of no value to you—your wife's winter coat or the kid's blue jeans—but they go for what means most to you.

A Brittany is born with the value judgment of a Gabor sister. Given a choice of several items, the Brittany instantly will choose the most valuable, most irreplaceable and reduce it to popcorn shards.

I have lived with Brittanies long enough now that penury is a constant companion. I have seen treasured family heirlooms, passed along from generation to generation, like my Fats Domino recording of "Love Me," treated the same way a lioness treats a juicy impala on Feast Day.

Brittanies practice their depredations by getting into the garbage, but they save their real game for the big-ticket items. For example, as I sweated copiously to build a house for Guff (who already had reduced a sleeping bag pad to filler for a high-jump pit and the goose down bag that went with it to something that looked like a massacre in the chicken house), I hung a brand-new, expensive hunting jacket on the gatepost.

I forgot it. Guff climbed atop the house I built for him, stretched out, and seized the sleeve in those iron jaws. When I reclaimed the jacket, it was a rag that would have been scorned in a hobo jungle.

Sure, every puppy chews up a shoe or two or discovers Mommy's new nightgown (direct from Frederick's of Hollywood that you were looking forward to seeing her model after sharing a bottle of a presumptuous little chablis) and reduces it to dipstick wipers.

But that is Class C ball in the world of the Brittany. The Brittany is a major league chewer, teeth gnashing like a scene from *The Texas Chainsaw Massacre*. He uses the occasional shoe as a canapé, a warm-up for larger things, like a pool table.

My wife had always wanted a pool table, no matter the reason. A game of eight ball was a vision she held in her mental hope chest, one that, being married to a penurious outdoor writer, she was not likely to realize.

But she came into a bit of money and, instead of buying a spare barrel of oatmeal for our puling bairns, she went downtown, clutching her entitlement, and shortly was followed home by a pool table.

About that time, I got Guff, an eleven-week-old French Brittany with big brown eyes and soft fur, like a cuddle-doll. He was my baby. He snuggled in my lap, looking up at me with eyes that promised unvarying fealty. Ah, he could do no wrong!

And Attila the Hun loved his mother . . .

Guff ate the pool table. I don't mean he ingested the entire thing, just the crucial parts of it, like the corners of the pockets, so that shooting a ball into a pocket was like driving a Volkswagen into a hangar for a Boeing 747. It takes some of the skill out of the game when you can use a fence post as a cue and shoot beach balls into the pockets with room to spare.

I have no idea how he was able to do this strange feat. Merely getting atop the table was a climbing feat equivalent to Norkey and Hillary scaling Everest. There was no way a pup his size could have climbed up there (and no sane reason one would even *want* to, for God's sake!). But he did, just as he quickly learned to climb out of a six-foot chain-link fence kennel like a capuchin monkey. Guff would beat me to the house after I locked him securely in the dog run.

I finally wired the top of the run. Even then he managed to cling by one paw while he worried a hole in the wire with another, then clambered up and out. It was a phenomenal feat, like something from a Bruce Willis movie, but I did not cheer for his heroics. I just applied more wire until he finally could not get out.

I'd always thought pouting was a human emotion, foreign to a dog, but Guff sulked like a kid denied a trip to Disneyland. The next time he got in the house for a visit he peed all over my thousand-dollar stereo speakers.

For all their transgressions, I love my Brittanies and have decided fatalistically that a major part of my income will go to replace shredded valuables.

How can I not love the Brit? Once, in a movie, a youngster whose father was thinking of marrying a socialite the kid didn't like said, "I don't trust her. She has narrow eyes." Perhaps somewhere there is a Brittany with narrow eyes, but I never met one. Instead, they are big eyed and those eyes are wet with simple affection. Brittany eyes plead, asking for any sign that they can leap on you with slurping tongue and wriggling pleasure.

That's a Brittany—vibrant affection.

Even as I write this, two of them are prancing about the room. One is batting an empty aluminum can with no more noise than is heard in the average foundry; the other rolled in a stinking dead fish earlier and still is socially unwelcome. Fortunately, this is a hunting camp and it is not mine, so the long-term effect of the stinking dog is not my problem.

Both dogs expect to climb on the bed after I have gone to sleep and make a place for themselves. It escapes me how a dog that weighs 40 pounds can dislodge a man who beefs in at 155. They sprawl over more territory than Montana. I wake up cold because they've squeezed me out from under the covers, like toothpaste from the tube. I'm half-hanging off the edge of the bed and these two dogs are snoring gently, twitching and reliving old hunts. This is life with Brittanies.

If they don't climb on the bed, they will spend the night chewing something (one night it was the power cord on the television set; it still is a miracle to me that I didn't wake up to fried Brittany). Considering the intense use to which a Brit puts his choppers, it's no wonder he needs regular dental care. My local pet supply pusher said, "You *must* take care of your dog's teeth!"

What I should have done was pull them, not take care of them, but instead I arrived home with a tool (cast of 24-karat gold judging from its cost) that looked like something you checker gunstocks with.

"This will remove that *terrible* tartar from your cherished doggie's teeth!" the guy exclaimed, looking like the actor on television who dresses in a white lab jacket and holds up a toothbrush and a tube of goo and implies that if you don't use the goo, your jaw will fall off and be consumed by maggots.

Have you ever tried chiseling plaque off the flashing teeth of a writhing Brittany? It's marginally easier than giving a vasectomy to a bobcat. It does no good to bellow "it's for your own good!" in the dog's ear, for bird dogs understand only "let's eat!" "birrrrd!" and "I'm gonna knock your thick head off!"

Once Guff lodged a shard of something he'd gnawed—possibly a suit of armor or a Sherman tank—between his gum and tooth and swelled up until he looked like a cantaloupe with ears. I told him it was a visitation from God, but talking theology to Brittanies is a waste of time. They only want to know when the next meal is.

No matter. The local vet doubles as a dog dentist and quickly put things right in Guff's mouth and wrong in my pocketbook. The vet and I have a cooperative agreement. He takes vacations and I pay for them.

One of his idylls came after Chubby tried to become the largest tenant on a stringer of trout. He ate the bait . . . which included a treble hook.

We were trout fishing with cheese balls ("oh, my God!" cry the purists) and when I laid aside the cheese bait in favor of a mammoth Rapala and turned my back for a moment, Chubby demonstrated the Brittany's inordinate love of cheese and ability to get into trouble with his mouth. "Oh, Chubbs! What have you done!" I cried, visualizing the hook caroming leopard-like through his digestive tract, ripping and clawing. He wriggled and slurped my ear.

I thought the vet was going to do the same when I presented the problem, for he hadn't had a good vacation for a long time and this obviously was going to go a long way toward propelling him to the carefree beaches in the Med or perhaps to whatever Central American country isn't at war.

The X-ray machines worked overtime, humming with the melodic sound of cash registers and, sure enough, there was the little treble hook, threading its way through Chubb's digestive system. "I've seen just about everything go through animals," the vet said, hastily qualifying his confidence with the assurance that he could perform incredibly expensive surgery if necessary. Much to his obvious disappointment (he had already booked first class and had to downgrade to coach), Chubbs eliminated his barbed visitor after about three days and began looking for more cheese balls.

Guff passed along not only his nose, which was acceptable in a bird dog, but also his chew genes. Two of his grandchildren managed to destroy their houses using not the dynamite, crowbars, and nine-pound-hammers of mus-

cular demolition teams but merely the few teeth that nature granted them. It's more than enough.

Recently somebody in the kennel managed to unhook
several connections of chain link, and I've found gnawed
pieces of chain link in the dog runs several times. Given
that dental determination, it's no wonder that doghouses
are at risk. I have designed doghouses that lacked only a
stereo and deep pile carpeting. They were double walled,
with paneling on the inside and foam insulation between
the walls. There was a wind baffle so the dogs could go
down a nice little hall, turn the corner, and be snug out
of the wind in a pile of prairie hay that smelled as sweet
as early summer.

So what did they do? They spent the long, cold days
of winter ripping out the paneling and shredding the
Styrofoam insulation. I looked down the hill to the
kennel one morning and saw the pen filled with what
appeared to be snow. It was blizzard weather, but the
only place that appeared to have drifts was inside the
dog run.

Not snow—Styrofoam insulation reduced to snowflake
size. A bitter north wind blew through the exposed cracks
and as the little devils shivered, I snarled, "You don't like
it? Grow hair!"

When we moved to the country, I built the doghouses
of six-inch cedar logs. That finally seemed to daunt the
Brits . . . but they have chewed a hole in the floor of one
house and are busy digging a tunnel, a scene straight out of
Stalag 17 or perhaps *Escape from Alcatraz*. The hell of it is
that if they did somehow manage to chew an escape hole

through the fence or tunnel under the house, they'd come up on the deck and snooze in the sun.

Not only do Brittanies use their teeth to shred your rainbow but they have a darker side. The bared fang is the Brit's primary weapon and a fearsome one at that. Males and females alike are prone to dispute territory with a frenzy of teeth.

Breaking up a dogfight is an art requiring NBA coordination, a working knowledge of dog psychology, and a bit of luck. In the throes of a fight, Ol' Happy has the instincts of a jackal at the kill and will savage the hand that feeds him with just as much contrition as a rampaging Mongol showed his victims.

I once broke up an intense dogfight by pouring beer down the noses of the combatants. Most dogs like beer, but not when it is injected intranasally. They broke off the fight wheezing and snorting and for a moment I thought they might gang up on *me*.

Another fight broke up spontaneously when the combatants toppled into a deep pool of water and suddenly found they couldn't breathe anymore. But you can't be sure there's going to be a convenient pool handy when Ginger and Buffy decide to dissect each other.

I stopped another fight by beating the dogs over the head with a jogging shoe. It took a lot of pounding until the dogs reasoned that the beating was more painful than the fight. It also subjected the shoe to more punishment than Michael Jordan in the NBA playoffs and ruined $20 of a $40 pair.

My favorite . . . well, no, most memorable . . . dogfight occurred on a quail hunt. One of the hunters had accused me of stretching the truth about the goofy things that happen to me in the boondocks.

And then he went quail hunting with me. We happened on a wounded deer. It was deer season and one fellow had a deer tag, so he hustled back to get his rifle, returned, and dispatched the deer. We field dressed it, not noticing the blooming feral glitter in the usually placid eyes of our Brittanies.

The fight erupted over a steaming pile of deer guts as two of the Brits decided to stake claim on the evening meal. I grabbed Chip's collar and thrust him behind me, both of us slipping and sliding and cursing in the slimy mass of internal organs (actually, I was the only one cursing).

The other Brittany backed off and I released my dog, only to realize I'd been cutting off his wind. Nearly unconscious, he staggered off with glassy eyes, the fight gone from him. If the other dog wanted the guts, he could have them. Geez!

So there we were with one dog semiconscious, another chagrined, several of us covered with internal organ slime and blood. Wide-eyed, the disbelieving hunter looked at me and said, "Well, I never believed all those stories, but I do now. I also am never going anywhere with you again."

Thus the Brittany goes through life, nose at the ready for quail and teeth at the ready for whatever will cost you money you can't afford. A pointer might poop on your shell vest; a setter gnaw on something cheap, like your shell vest or his food dish. But the Brit goes right for the pocketbook.

I believe that if he realized everything dear to you is in a safe deposit box at the corner bank, he would penetrate the vault door quicker than a double dose of nitroglycerine, find your safe deposit box, puncture it like an armor piercing tank round, and eat your will or maybe the tapioca mine stocks that promise someday to make you a millionaire.

The Brittany, soft, sweet, magic nose . . . and a frenzy of teeth.

God love him!

SIX

It Begins with Puppies

Chaps was half cocker, half springer. She was black-and-white and freckle pawed. Her name came from that of a dog in Mary O'Hara's book *My Friend Flicka*.

I was six years old and she was my first dog, a gift from my parents who probably thought that having a dog would teach me responsibility. Instead she taught me to cry and swear when she chewed up a model Focke Wulf fighter airplane that I had worked on for many days. I had patiently glued the balsa wood struts and braces together, painstakingly covered the thing with tissue paper and, doped it so the paper would stretch tight over the braces and struts and look like a real Focke Wulf fighter.

I finished it one evening after school. I had waited all day through endless, boring classes at Chicago's Arthur Dixon Elementary School to run home and put the finishing touches on my Focke Wulf.

The Focke Wulf had the black Iron Cross insignia of the German air force and, while I was a loyal American, it was a neater looking airplane than the British Spitfire or the American P-38. This was during World War II and I was all for the Spitfires and P-38s shooting down every Focke Wulf that crossed their paths . . . just not mine.

I liked the symmetry of that cross. The British rondell and the American star were okay, but those Germans knew how to decorate an airplane, even if we did try to send them all down in flames.

Chaps, either a superpatriotic dog or just exhibiting her spaniel chew genes, had different ideas. I left my model on the floor, and as I ate my mother's meatloaf, Chaps ate my Focke Wulf. I found it shredded and I raged at the dog and cried and was inconsolable. Chaps merely looked puzzled. I called her a son of a bitch (when my parents weren't around, ignoring the genetic realities). Maybe we should have inducted Chaps into the U.S. Army Air Corps and let her chew our way to aerial superiority.

Chaps was supposed to be my dog, but she quickly attached herself to my father. I was a little kid and knew nothing about dogs (except that they ate airplanes). She was the first dog in my life and she was there for sixteen years, until I married and became a father. That's a considerable chunk of a person's life to spend with any animal.

Given a normal life span, you'll outlive your dogs. It's the reality of dog ownership, sadder for the owner than the dog because the dog doesn't know but the owner does. Dogs are creatures of now; we are cursed with foresight.

Since Chaps, I've entertained a succession of puppies—several collies and then a long string of Brittanies, both American and French. I've grown to cherish that fleeting time of puppyhood. I just don't build model airplanes around them.

Puppyhood is so brief. It's comparable to the brief existence of a mayfly. Mayflies shuck their larval coat, spread their wings, fly with primordial joy to the light, mate, and then fall to earth and die.

A puppy comes into the world as a struggling, helpless handful, eyes squinched shut and soaked with birth fluids. But all too soon it is leggy, bumptious, and awkward. And then it's grown and not a puppy anymore except in memory.

Two months—that's about it. They're born and eight weeks later they have gone home with someone else. We've raised six litters of French Brittanies. Puppies helped put our son Andy through college, but even as they paid for his schooling, each one that went away with strangers ripped a little piece out of my heart.

For those seven or eight weeks, they were ours. We helped them into the world, watched them blindly nurse, switched them around on the faucets to make sure everyone got a healthy dose of mother's milk, saw the first glimmer of eyeball, struggled with them as they tried to get their feet under them, watched their shaky first steps, laughed as they skidded through the gruel of puppy chow, held them close and smelled a sweet-sour milk aroma, watched them toddle on still rebellious legs to investigate plants and smells and a strange and wonderful world.

We have lived with these little morsels of life and when they leave it is as if a part of us has gone too. Fortunately for them, an eight-week-old puppy has not seriously bonded with mother, nor sibling, nor Big Thing That Is There. So it's not so traumatic for the puppy to be jerked from a warm pile of puppies to a new home . . . but it's tough on old people like me who cry helplessly at Lassie movies.

Our kennel has been half-populated with leftover dogs. Chubby was the last of a litter and I could not bear to part with him. Tess was a flake, a puppy who peed all over herself if you spoke harshly to her—how could I sell a neurotic dog to someone else? Pucques was a he when buyers wanted a she.

Scruffy was too . . . well, scruffy as a puppy and I figured no one would pick such a seedy-looking mutt and they didn't. Jay was a beautiful pup, but everyone wanted females and besides he and Andy fell in love.

Of them all, Guff was the only one acquired by purchase. He was the founder of the line; all the rest have been home-grown.

We chose Pepper, Dacques, Missy, and Flick from among various litters. Pepper was Guff's daughter and destined to be the den mother of the rest. Dacques was her firstborn and Andy picked him as his best friend with four legs. Flick was Guff's replacement, Pepper's grandson. Missy was Tess's daughter and her replacement as the resident fecund female.

But chosen or left over, they each have carved out a spot in our affections, have earned their keep in the field. They're friends, pets, whatever . . . but they are bird dogs and the hunting time of the year is when our relationship is in full flower.

The nice IRS lady fixed me with a gimlet eye during an audit and said, "What is this $1,500 for dog supplies?" I explained that I am an outdoor writer and I write about dogs, and they are therefore my tools, just as a carpenter has his hammers and saws. She said, "I don't much like dogs," and I began to wonder if federal prison mattresses were any lumpier than mine.

"Well, I suppose anyone with seven dogs isn't doing it as a hobby," she said, allowing the expense. Hobby? There's no box on the income tax form for "obsession." That's what it is, this ferment of man and dog in the field.

Game bird hunting is simple. You walk around until something shootable flies and you shoot it and take it home and eat it.

Sure. But if that was all there was to it, why not shoot a round of sporting clays and stop for a bucket of Kentucky Fried on the way home? That would be a far more predictable event than hunting, a known outcome. Hunting always carries a question mark.

Two things make the difference: the dog and the chase, the feeling that just around that sprout of sumacs is a covey, crouched and fluttery with apprehension and that your four-legged buddy will work them with skill and grace.

I know a few bird hunters who hunt without dogs and claim they don't need them. They don't feel they are missing the essence of the bird hunt. But I can't believe they have trudged behind the bobbing butt of an eager bird dog, seen one leaned into a wall of bird stink, quivering and walleyed, had a dog miraculously find a cripple far from where it fell, had a dog rest its muzzle on a knee come night and ask only to be touched.

Anyone who experiences those things and does not become owned by a dog simply does not deserve to be with a dog.

Getting a bird dog is like getting married except that, the way things are today, the contract lasts longer. Ideally, man and dog have a working arrangement of at least a decade and often longer. These days marriages that last ten years are an anomaly.

But beyond length of service, man and dog share affection and understanding. Dogs don't ask why; they only ask to go. Psychologists use terms like "bonding" and "socialization," but I prefer "love" and "trust." Better words.

I remember the litters, not with any sharp clarity, but as a time of sweet innocence. Each time we had a litter, I thought the same thing—that if I could, I'd have kept the whole bunch and if I were God, they'd perennially be seven weeks old, fuzzy, feisty, and fun. But I'm not God and they were picked off, one by one, and then they were gone and all we had was a memory of warm wriggling bodies and wet tongues and sharp little teeth . . . and an ache that lingered.

It's not as if they died. In fact, they brought sunshine to other homes and lighted the lives of other hunters. But those hunters aren't me and I'll always miss our little guys.

Pepper delivered the first litter when Andy was barely a teenager. She was his dog and she consented to a planned liaison with a Continental type, a Parisian Brit with a definite Chevalier rakishness about him. I expected him to start whining "thank heaven for little dogs . . ." In fifty-two days, she delivered seven lusty pups.

There was so much champion blood on both sides that the pups should have been designated "Ch." by birthright, like conceding a six-inch putt. For all their dogs' royal genetics, five of the new owners were going to have a hard time convincing their doubting hunting pards that these really were Brittanies because they were black-and-white, not the traditional orange- or liver-and-white of the familiar American Brittany.

Dog breeding/raising was a bit of a miracle for us. We aren't in the business. I know a few kennel owners and marvel at their attitude toward the dogs they breed. It's a livestock business and the dogs, while the breeders brag about them and have a certain affection for some of them, still are treated as animated tools. They aren't considered four-legged people.

It's not as if I live in the kennel with my dogs. They have concrete runs and their own houses, and they spend much of their time in the kennel. But I also have shared tent space with them and when we're far north in the grouse woods, I don't object when one hops on the bed and sleeps against my knee when the October cold invades the cabin.

It was years before I got portable kennels for the vehicle. I somewhat enjoyed Guff's eager attention next to me in the front as he left nose prints all over the passenger side of the windshield.

I enjoyed him spying crows on the wing and bounding to the back of the car as we passed so he could keep them in sight. I enjoyed watching him bristle at cows in the fields along the road. And I enjoyed having his warm body snuggled against my leg as we headed home in the night after a long quail hunt.

These are things that I remember, which means they must have been special. Perhaps they were insignificant and ephemeral moments in a lifetime . . . but why do I remember them if they weren't important?

Guff was my friend. I mourn far more for him than he would for me because I am more complex. But on some gut level we were the same. We cherished the same things and we bonded on some elemental level where all creatures are equal. Some people have sublimated that level so they can't reclaim it. They feel they have evolved or risen or whatever, but I think they have merely boxed themselves in.

They'll never know the quiet pleasure of a dog leaning against them at the end of a long day. This is a strong pleasure, one that shoulders other, more transitory pleasures aside. I'd hate not to know this pleasure.

Part of the fun of each new litter is giving the individual pups a name. It's not the name their new owners will use (although a few have), but it's our reading of them (thus "Scruffy," which I doubt is a name any owner who just plunked down several hundred dollars would give his new acquisition).

Our names aren't elaborate kennel names like Ithaca du Calembour (Pepper) or Anat du Buisson de Choisel (Baron, her Gallic godsend) or even a call name like Speck or Spot or whatever. The names have been chosen according to their peculiarities. There was Big Head, who looked deformed for a while until he grew into the head he'd been born with.

By the time he left us he'd turned into a handsome, lusty seven-week-old bruiser whose body was expanding to meet his head. We carefully refrained from calling him Ol' Big Head in front of the guy who was shelling out the bucks to buy him.

Then there was Esther, the midsized black-and-white female who pranced around at the edge of the lake for a few seconds and then dived in with a Labrador-like leap that carried her all of six inches. Esther Williams, what else?

Chubby was a round dog, first in line at the food dish. His mouth was his distinction, for he also was the barkingest of the bunch. He looked like Humpty-Dumpty.

The Frecklepaws were two little pups, one male, one female. They were inseparable and as alike as could be. The little female was petite and sweet, runt of the litter, but giving nothing away in feist to her larger brethren.

Both Frecklepaws were people dogs. The whole group was, but the FPs courted people and wriggled with delight when they were noticed. They appeared to want most to crawl inside your mouth and down your throat and be a part of you. Fastest tongues in the West.

I called the other pup Little Guffy because he so much reminded me of my beloved Guff at the same age—same feisty personality, same bounce. He never ran, waddled, walked anywhere. He bounded. He invariably leaped before he looked. Brick walls were made for running through. Guts of a middle linebacker, size of a 103-pound-class wrestler. He's the one who caught my heart. He's the one I dreaded sending off.

Seven puppies take a bunch of room, not to mention a bunch of food, shots, heartworm pills, and dog vitamins, all of which goes into creating waste matter in staggering proportions. If it is true that under the right conditions sewage can be used to create methane gas for energy, I could have heated Buffalo, New York, for an entire record-breaking winter.

In addition to the problem of sewage disposal, keeping puppies and older dogs in harmony takes diplomacy that would baffle Henry Kissinger. Adult dogs are Mother Russia and the pups are satellite republics when it comes to amicability in the pen. The first two big dogs grab the two houses and any puppy brash enough to stick a paw inside gets whomped.

So, the big dogs were relegated to one house where two, but not three, could sleep in relative harmony. Ginger and Pepper would sleep together all right, or Ginger and Guff . . . but not Ginger, Guff, and Pepper, even though the house is large enough for all three.

Pepper, who can lick her weight in wildcats and regularly savages Ginger, for some reason turned demure and Ginger ousted her from her own house. She was as forlorn as little Mary Pickford in a silent tearjerker. One night she stood in the rain until I struggled out of bed at 3 a.m., sloshed down the hill in a pair of shorts and nothing else, stepped in puppy poop barefooted, tried to ignore the excited clawings of more than fifty puppy toenails, as I let Pepper out and put her in the garage.

Had anyone talked to me about emotion and puppies at that moment, I would have displayed quite a strong emotion and the language to go with it.

Then the litter began to be picked off by buyers. Intellectually, I knew we couldn't keep them. Three adult dogs (at the time) was stretching it and Andy was keeping a pup. My wife's tolerance Plimsoll line had submerged at two Brittanies a long time before. We were fast approaching the "me or the dogs" stage.

I let the prospective buyers talk, listening for telltale personality clues. One buyer sounded all right, but he nailed down his claim when he started raving about his eighteen-pound female Brittany who "rides in the front seat with me and looks at everything." The love was apparent in his voice, as was his respect for the tiny dog who refused to concede size to any of the other dogs in the field. When he asked for the little female Freck, I knew it was a marriage made in heaven.

Then there was the guy who called wanting a stud dog for his kennel to breed odd-color Brittanies. "The market's about shot for orange-and-whites down here," he said. He didn't know it, but the market was shot for him with me, too. I'll be damned if any of our puppies ever goes to a livestock breeder. I told him the pups all were accounted for.

The little guys were individuals and they belonged with individuals, not with a herd of other dogs, shut up in runs all day, every day, and rarely if ever hunted, trained, or loved. No way.

Ol' Big Head went north to Wisconsin, headed for a career as a grouse/woodcock dog. Then a fellow from

Memphis, quail country, chose Esther and won my approval (I felt like a doting father critically sizing up prospective sons-in-law) when he cuddled her close to his face and murmured, "Oh, she's beautiful!" She was.

There were four left—the two Frecklepaws, Chubby, and Little Guffy. One Frecklepaw went to Virginia and the other to Texas, a final and heart-wrenching separation for them because they had played and slept together, constant companions. Or at least that's the way I pictured it. Maybe it wasn't. I don't know. Snoopy and his brother, Spike, were separated at the Daisy Hill Puppy Farm and now are a continent apart and still think of each other. But then they're cartoon dogs.

"O, native land, no more to thee shall I return . . ." That's what Aida sings in Verdi's opera of the same name. I can hear, in my imagination, Esther or Little Guffy or the Frecklepaws howling a canine version of Verdi in a lonesome kennel far away.

In one day, we stuck three on airplanes headed for places I'd never see, and then we were down to two puppies, the one Andy was keeping (still without a name other than "My Guy") and Chubby, roly-poly as ever, the little round dog. He looked like Fats Domino, every bit as endearing as the rotund rocker. Marty and I took Little Guffy and the two Frecklepaws to the airport.

I didn't sleep much the night before because Little Guffy was leaving. I couldn't help thinking of him as "my dog" even though he'd been spoken for. I didn't talk on the way to the airport and when my thoughts turned to the feisty little pup with the big eyes and the face that would melt glaciers, I'd have to bite my lip.

You're a big guy now, I told myself. *Pushing fifty-two years old and you act like a little kid.*

Go to hell, I told me.

I was all right until a burly freight handler who looked like Jesse Ventura grabbed a puppy carrier in each hand and hauled them up to the loading dock. Little Guffy was in one of the carriers. My eyes brimmed. "You'll have to go in," I told Marty, my voice tight. "I can't do it."

So she went inside to make the shipping arrangements while I went over to the loading dock and opened the cage door and let Little Guffy crawl out in my lap. I held him close, knowing it was the last time I'd ever see him, and felt his wavy, soft hair against my cheek, his sweet puppy breath in my nose. He licked at my face and wriggled happily, sure that now he was out of that damn awful cage, I was going to take him home where he belonged.

But I wasn't, of course, and all too soon it was time to put him, uncomprehending and resisting, back in the cage, and walk off without looking back, tears running down my face.

When we got home, I went to the kennel. Where the kennel run had seemed a furry carpet of puppies only yesterday, now it was coldly empty and the two pups remaining were dwarfed by it.

I opened the gate and got Chubby out. He was his usual cheerful, chunky self and he found a niche in my lap and curled up there, happy only to be with somebody.

This was a dog I hadn't paid much attention to, wrapped up as I was with Little Guffy. He was a middle child, ignored in the shuffle, and the more I looked at him, the more I saw what an injustice that was. He had a charming face, button-bright eyes, and spunky personality.

He'd been the first one to chase a ball and retrieve it and he brought it to hand and released it with a gentle mouth, boding well for the future. He took to the water like an otter, splashing happily in the pond while his littermates tiptoed nervously at the water's edge. He'd taken a dove I'd brought home and carried it worriedly around the yard, not sure what he was supposed to be doing but caught in the grip of something powerful and irresistible.

There were a couple of people interested in a puppy and here was the last available one. I looked at Chubby, feeling that old familiar glow start up. Something there said My Dog, and I knuckled his fluffy ears and he gnawed at my hand.

I went in the house and wrote letters to the potential customers telling them the dogs all had been sold and I was sorry. I told Marty that we were keeping Chubby and when she looked at me, the beginning protest died on her lips. She wins nine out of ten confrontations, but she knew this was one she wouldn't win.

Five dogs in a kennel built for maybe three. Vet bills to stagger the pocketbook of a Rockefeller. A third doghouse imperative before the snow flies. The demand of training this new responsibility and still finding time to hunt the other dogs.

An irrational, irresponsible decision, but one that demanded to be made. In the immortal words of Scarlett O'Hara, "I'll think about it tomorrow."

SEVEN

Ma Barker

She tackled old age the same way she'd tackled her other life stages—with a no-nonsense, focused intensity that brushed distractions aside.

For Pepper, a distraction was anything she didn't want to do, like mind or honor or die. She always had an agenda and, like a corporate shark, she went after it. She was a Donald Trumpette.

Pepper beat all the canine actuarial odds. If the old rule of thumb of one dog year equaling seven human ones, Pepper got to be 105 years old. At that age, dog or human, you figure to wake up dead some morning. Pepper couldn't hear (or didn't choose to); she had cloudy eyeballs and she was portly, but inside that geriatric exterior beat the heart of a six-month-old puppy, tasting the world as if it were T-bone.

One morning when she was fifteen, five Canada geese landed on the pond and seven dogs raced out on the dock to goggle at them. Pepper, infinitely smarter than the rest, circled the pond to the far side where the geese were paddling sedately, safe in their distance from the hysterical dock dogs.

She came out of the grass like a black panther, albeit a bit slower than in her salad days, and the alarmed geese took to the air in a fluster with the dog right behind them. Pepper's only shortcoming was that she could not fly or we would have had goose for dinner.

She was convinced for years that she could catch one of the big birds that visit our pond every spring. That she did not do so was not even a faint abrasion on her iron confidence. She was the most confident creature who ever lived, and the most willful. Failure was not in her vocabulary. Anything that resembled failure was merely a temporary setback.

Pepper may have had cat genes in her, for she sometimes seemed alien, operating on a schedule that might have been written in a distant galaxy. Humans were curious creatures, somewhat amusing, but nothing to get fussy about. We fulminated and dramatized, but it was all sound and fury, signifying nothing. I am not a permissive parent with our dogs and will resort to whipping when the transgressions cross certain boundaries that both the dog and I know.

But with Pepper a whipping was no more effective than hymn singing and the laying on of hands. She decided early on that the fun of dog sin was worth corporal punishment.

She usually did not deliberately disobey. Often she was as sweet as maple sap, but she was focused on her impenetrable goals with the determination that allows the creation of works of art, great books, and, probably, tyrants and dictators.

Pepper was the mother of Dacques and Chubby from the first of her four litters, and Tess from her last. She was the grandmother of Pucques, Flick, Jay, Scruffy, and Missy. But if you're expecting a grandmother with a twinkle in her eye, all crinoline and lace and lavender scent, think again.

We called her Ma Barker, a clever wordplay on her dogness, but also indicative of her personality. Ma Barker was the infamous elder of a gang of outlaws in the Roaring Twenties, a fearsome old bag with four sons, all of whom died violently, and who herself died in a machine gun shootout with the FBI.

Pepper was not likely to run afoul of the FBI, but dog crimes were her nature (i.e., failing to come because she simply didn't want to, getting into the trash, failing to honor points, and other bird dog felonies).

She was scolded and whipped for raiding the kitchen trash for fifteen years and she knew right from wrong . . . but she still headed for the trash basket as soon as she was let in. She decided that no punishment we could devise was horrific enough to spoil the pleasure of dragging out meat wrappers and other enticing detritus.

Occasionally she would swallow some indigestible substance and I would have to pull strips of plastic wrapper from her rear end with a pair of pliers. It was not among my favorite things to do.

Pepper was the Barbara Walters of dogdom, the nosiest creature I've ever known. She should have been born human and become a reporter. *New York Times? Wall Street Journal?*

Naah—more like the *National Enquirer.* Not only was Pepper nosy; she had low tastes. She thrived on gunk. Rabbit droppings were mutt M&Ms to her. The old description of "leaner than a junkyard dog" wouldn't have applied—she would have gotten as fat as a slop-fed hog.

Let in the house, Pepper made herself at home by immediately checking every trash basket in the house. The first stop was the one in the kitchen because it held food residue. But, left unchecked, she was like a wildfire. She spread through the house, tipping over trash baskets, chewing up the tasty morsels therein.

Pepper was a trial and a curse. And she was fourteen before I finally admired her without reservation. She had mothered nearly thirty children, most of whom turned out wonderfully well.

Pepper was the toughest creature I've ever encountered. She didn't just endure pain—she ignored it. Once she ripped her belly open, probably on a barbed wire fence. Yip or complain? No, not Pepper. We didn't even know she was hurt until we accidentally saw the gaping wound. Hell, *she* didn't even know she was hurt.

She had no fear of anything, which meant we had to be her watchdogs—in her mind a speeding car wouldn't dare hit Pepper. As I said before, she once made the UPS truck wait for five minutes while she finished relieving herself in the middle of the road. She never even bothered to look over her shoulder at the looming truck just behind her. The driver, a bird hunter, thought it was funny. Someone else might not have.

Pepper was somewhat smarter than I am, a fact I am reluctant to admit but which became readily obvious over the years. She would have sent any dog trainer into retirement. She always did what she damn well pleased. And don't give me any of this "you should have let her know who was boss." Pepper knew who was the boss ever since she was born.

She was.

When she got to an age when most bird dogs are dead, I figured she would be prancing on her grave. Death? Just another looming presence trying to tell her what to do. She would survive somehow—maybe as a tornado.

Pepper was the pick of the litter. Guff, my longtime friend and confidant, had a licit affair with Gypsy, a sultry tricolor temptress owned by the late Dave Meisner, founder of *Gun Dog* magazine. The result of this one-day stand was a litter of eight puppies.

Andy Vance then was twelve years old and my hunting partner. He had a nice double-barrel, shell vest, and cap, everything the bird hunter needs except his own dog.

So the pick of the litter was his. We watched the puppies wander around Dave's yard and I suggested several good-looking ones, puppies I would have picked. Andy was like Pepper—you can tell him what to do, but he makes the final decision on whether he's going to do it or not. Andy took his time.

Then he settled on an unprepossessing, almost totally black little female—perhaps the last pup I would have selected. But she had picked up an empty soft drink can and carried it around and she was still awake and alert when the rest of the litter had drifted off to puppy sleep and she had investigated Andy as if she were checking his credit references.

He said, "I'll take her. She likes me."

And fourteen years later, they still liked each other. No . . . they loved each other. "She's my doll," Andy said simply.

Pepper showed puppy spunk all her life. She'd drop to her elbows, butt up, in the play posture. "Come on, let's romp!" she would demand, peering up at you through eyes gone cloudy with cataracts. Age? That's for old dogs. Let's go chase rabbits.

And rabbits Pepper chased. She was an unregenerate rebel since birth. God, I loved her even as she flat made me mad. I refused to take her along on hunts for years because she would drive me to distraction with her ill manners in the field.

Gradually I began to empathize with the little black dog. I realized she couldn't help it. She was so competitive that if she wasn't first in line, she was compelled to creep until she *was* first. And she was in the field with her children and grandchildren and grandnephews. What could those wet-eared upstarts possibly know that she didn't?

Pepper had puppies the way most people have breakfast. Birth pain was, if it existed, a minor inconvenience. I midwifed one litter and Pepper bore her eight children without a whimper. It was a blip in the day.

Andy oversaw the first litter. Pepper had several puppies, then went to the door as if she had to go out. She had another in the backyard. She delivered a litter of eight puppies in less than two hours. Hell, she had better things to do than lie around groaning and giving birth.

Pepper was a wonderful mother if you don't count motherhood as great love and chicken soup. She gave birth to them, nursed them, raised them to a point where the humans could take over with grueled puppy chow, then she said, "Okay, enough already. I have rabbits to chase. Call me if there are problems."

As a parent of five children, I admired her outlook on parenting. She did what she had to do superlatively and then she said, "You're on your own." Sink or swim. Three of her kids wound up as kennel mates. She gave them The Look.

Pepper had The Look all her life. Over time it lost some of its effectiveness, but it still was impressive. Dacques, her firstborn son, is built like a pulling guard. He can run through brick walls and he's never lost a fight. He is Doc the Jock. He is burly and tough and would bite the ear off Mike Tyson.

But Pepper merely had to give him The Look and Dacques would slink off to a corner of the kennel and sit with his back to her. It was not just a female-male thing, either. Her daughter, Tess, became the resident Brood Bitch, but Tess would no more have thought of challenging Pepper as Boss Bitch than I would think of telling a Marine drill sergeant that I'd rather not do those pushups and besides, he's ugly.

There were no growls, no bared teeth associated with The Look. It was a stare that withers flowers and makes chain link begin to melt. Professional assassins have The Look. Clint Eastwood has The Look. Pepper had The Look. Even I got uneasy when Pepper gave me The Look, which she did when I commanded her to do something she didn't want to do.

So she was my canine cross to bear. Until the epiphany. "Epiphany" is a word meaning revelation or discovery. Our epiphany with Pepper came on a late-season quail hunt on the back side of Nowhere.

Andy, Pepper's nominal boss, and I were slogging along behind five Brittanies, all related to Pepper, all subservient to her. We figured that since it was late in the season and we'd slaked our bloodlust, we would take the whole gang of dogs and surround 'em.

But we hadn't found a covey in three hours of hunting. And then, along the bank of a creek, far back in the brush and horseweeds, we got a point.

It was not Dacques, nor Chubby, the elder statesdogs of the kennel. It was not Flick, the shining light of the males, nor Tess, the Wonderdog.

It was Pepper, first in line where she had imagined she belonged for so many years. She was locked down tighter than a bull's behind in fly time. She was lost in a hypnotic world that only bird dogs know. "Pepper's got 'em," Andy said, his voice hesitant, for he has lived with her all these years too. "Pepper's got 'em."

The covey came up in a flurry and we shot a couple of birds in the confusion and the tangle and . . . and . . . Pepper found the first dead bird and, for the first time in fourteen years, she picked it up and brought it to Andy. Pepper not only had made the point, but she also made the retrieve.

We were on opposite sides of a deep ditch, but Andy looked across at me, with the bird in his hand and the little black dog at his side, and the gulf that exists between father and son, between one era and another, between your dog and mine, the unseen gulf and the actual one, shrank and I was with him and his fine little dog and I did not yell at Pepper nor chastise her for trash grabbing or rabbit running after that moment.

I cherished the little dog with The Look and wished I could be just like her—renegade, rebel, the marcher to a different drummer. Everyone needs something like Pepper in his life—something to make the take-no-crap genes vibrate.

I'd hoped she would live to a hundred years and on her hundredth birthday, she would plop down in the play posture and bark demandingly: "Hey, let's go chase some rabbits!"

She passed her fifteenth birthday and then she simply vanished one sunny early summer day. She'd been having fainting spells but had recovered from them. Perhaps she went on one of her patrols of our property, making sure it was safe from Canada geese, and without fuss laid down and died.

We never found her.

I choose to think she chased a phantom rabbit into whatever future lies ahead for old dogs.

EIGHT

Feel-Good Dog

Chubby joined the kennel by default. His mother and brother were hand-picked by Andy, and his Grandpa Guff was hand-picked by me. They were wanted dogs.

Chubby was picked by fate.

Andy fretted over a name for his pick, Chubby's brother, a burly black-and-white male. He finally settled on what would be Doc if the pup were an American breed, but is spelled Dacques, a tribute to his French heritage.

Chubby got his name because he was, well, as my hunting buddy Spence Turner refers to himself, "rotund." The little dog never met a food dish he didn't empty.

He is no longer fat. Age has leaned him, but his fluffy coat still makes him look portly. Chubby is my feel-good dog. "He makes me feel good," I tell people, and they look at me the way people look at me when I ride the shopping cart downhill to the car, as if I haven't quite grown up and need to.

Chubby and Dacques have snarled at each other their entire lives. Trash talkin'. Woofin'. It's sibling rivalry in full flower.

Dacques was the firstborn of Pepper's puppies, and Chubby came along later in the evening, but not much later because Pepper was fed up with carrying around that sack of pups and delivered all seven within two hours.

Dacques always has been the jock of the litter, a chesty French Brittany with the gee-whizzy enthusiasm of a high school fullback. My wife claims he has a set of weights stashed in the doghouse and he works out at night, a dozen reps of curls and presses, a few lifts, a half-hundred snarls at Chubby. Picking up Dacques is like picking up a sack of concrete that has gotten wet and set. He is a fur-covered boulder.

Dacques has made love; Chubby never has. Dacques strides up to a female like an NFL pulling guard in a bar, hormones dripping off him; Chubby is tentative but inquisitive, as if scenting new game—he's ready for action but not sure what the action is.

Chubby is stocky and sweet-tempered. His fur is soft and curly (any woman would kill for his natural curl). Dacques runs like a rocking horse, tight-muscled and jointed; Chubby is more conventional, slower and more methodical.

In their salad days, they swept most bird fields pretty clean. Now they've grown old and the desire is there, but their genetics are letting them down. Dacques is hobbled by front leg arthritis and Chubby's tendons have gotten like mine, old rubber that has lost its snap.

They seem to pay no attention to each other as they hunt, but if you plotted their route on graph paper, it would have a geometrical symmetry. I don't know if they communicate when they hunt. There's no visible evidence. Perhaps it is an unspoken communication of the blood, a telepathic bond steeped in their very marrow. They don't need to talk. They just *know*.

When they're in the field, they are the soul of co-operation, but that sweet teamwork vanishes when they're home in the kennel, especially when it's meal-time. Then they growl at each other, begin to posture and threaten. They snarl, lift ruff fur, and semaphore white-of-eye messages.

Not all the time, but when there is something at stake, like food or me. Of the two, I am the better prize. Purina Hi-Pro is good, but daddy is better. Chubby usually starts it; he is the more emotionally fragile, ever afraid someone will take me away from him.

The food is always available—there are three self-feeders in the dog pen, so they each could have one, with one left over, but whichever one starts eating first spends as much time growling at his brother as he does eating. They stick their heads in the small opening, muzzle to muzzle, and the barrel of the feeder serves as a sound chamber. The rumble is like distant thunder.

They'll stand shoulder to shoulder, heads lowered, mouthing the most awful canine threats. Neither wants to back down. Matter of pride. Finally the tension slackens and they forget the hoorah and wind up sleeping with each other. It never quite comes to physical combat. They're like diplomats rattling sabers at a public forum, all bombast and posture. Any United Nations delegate would recognize them instantly.

In a way it's a nice feeling to be the object of their affection. Everyone wants to be wanted. But I don't want to be the instigator of violence. It's no fun standing in the middle of a duel, even if it's a duel over me. I try to explain that they are co-equal in my affections; that I do not favor one over the other—but they're like brothers anywhere: "Dad *always* liked you better than he liked me!"

When we sleep together, which happens on the road, Chubby and Dacques vie for a spot next to me. Chubby is convinced he is my face dog, destined to lie close to my cheek where I can feel his soft night breath on my ear and the curl of his neck on my cheek.

Dacques would like to be a face dog but has resigned himself to being a lower-body dog. He presses close to my leg (it's like lying next to a statue fallen over on its side). And he and Chubby growl at each other over my prone body while I try to conjure images of fabled starlets whose inhibitions have fled at the sight of me.

"You let your dogs sleep with you!" cry the owners of bird dogs around the country. I will be castigated by those who consign their dogs to a cold kennel come night, stuck usually with another stinking dog in wet straw, but that's me.

I've spent quite a few nights in an RV, with a radio softly playing vintage Mozart, a glass of dew collected in

Scotland, and a couple of brothers drowsing in the warmth. I read a good book for a while and let the music and the warmth loosen the tight muscles of six hours in the boonies, and then the boys and I stretch and head for bed.

Say what you will, it's comforting to have a warm body next to you in the small hours. Maybe grandma Raquel Welch would be better than Dacques or Chubby, but I've had to settle for the brothers so far (I'm not giving up hope on Raquel because I'm a bird hunter and true bird hunters always know there is a covey in the next brush patch).

Sibling rivalry is a ferocious thing. Our two oldest sons, J.B. and Eddie, once got into a fistfight in our living room. Eddie hit J.B. in the nose, which started to bleed copiously, and J.B., swinging wildly, flung gobbets of blood on the wall. It looked like a scene from a slasher movie, but as long as they were still standing and cussing, I stayed out of the way. Sibling rivalry is nothing to get in the middle of.

After all, there is the lesson of Cain and Abel. But Eddie was best man at J.B.'s wedding a few years later and J.B. recently returned the favor for Eddie. Underneath the vengeful peaks and valleys of their younger days was a transcendent love.

Perhaps Dacques and Chubby have a similar emotion for each other. They wouldn't call it love if they could, dogs not being sentimental like people. A friend has pondered the difference between people, who are linear in their thinking, and dogs, who are episodic: people think of time as an evenly flowing river (and we know its source and its fearsome debouchment); dogs as a series of pools.

A human knows when hunting season ends and feels the weight of the time between seasons. But a dog knows only that it has been hunting season and maybe it will be today. A dog does not know of encroaching age or approaching death. It knows today and maybe a little bit of yesterday, but nothing of tomorrow.

Dacques and Chubby know "this food is mine, sucker, so keep your chops out of it!" except when the skirmish is over. Then the insult is forgotten and it's time to sleep and dream of rabbits chased and quail pointed. There is a simplicity in this lifestyle that precludes worry over illness and death and where the next meal is coming from. I envy this simple outlook.

Perhaps because we live six or seven times as long as a dog, we pay for it with awareness. We span the time between the flivver and the Impala, the Jenny and the jet, whereas a dog may live only the life of the family car.

Most people wouldn't trade the ability to reason in depth and even to worry or to fear the unknown for a dog's simple frame of reference. But there are plenty of times in the still of the night when ghosts press close that being Chubby or Dacques seems pretty attractive. They're the ones twitching with joyously fevered dreams while I lie awake and think of demons.

You never know what to expect with brothers. They reinforce each other and instead of doubling the potential for trouble, they seem to square it. It was ever thus with J.B. and Eddie who caromed through their teenage years as if dedicated to making their mother and me old well ahead of schedule.

Both survived that maelstrom and now are solid citizens. I've always loved them; now I even like them.

Dacques and Chubby may reach that period of emotional maturity where they recognize each other's rights and do not trespass, although as they topped thirteen years, I was still waiting for it.

We moved to the country in the mid-1990s and since becoming a country dog, Chubby has caught and eaten a squirrel. They both caught and killed a young raccoon and a young skunk, and Chubby discovered and shared with Dacques a brood of young turkeys. Each caught and retrieved one to my son Andy, who could only shake his head. They were wonderfully pleased that they had found and brought home these big game birds without assistance from me.

That the birds were out of season and too young were details not material to a dog's episodic life. No point in Ol' Linear Me explaining that if they had let those turkeys grow up they might have been trophy gobblers responding to my call and that if the conservation officer had happened by I'd have had some explaining to do.

Dacques and Chubby are hunting animals . . . as I am. I wouldn't chase down and eat a raw squirrel, but I shoot them out of the trees and make Biglersville stew of them. I wouldn't shoot a baby turkey, but I long for the moment when the little guy develops a beard and a deep yodel and comes to my call.

There's no basic difference between the dogs drowsing in the kennel and me. We live to hunt and we love to eat what we kill. The dogs are mannered enough not to eat what I kill in front of them, but they figure that if they ice it, it's supper.

And there really isn't much difference in brothers, be they Brittanies or Vances. When all the petty differences are solved, it's time to throw your arm/paw around the other guy's shoulders and face the world.

Of all our dogs, Chubby, I think, has been the most dear. Guff was my best friend for his years with us, but Chubby didn't realize or care that he might be number 2. He lived and lives to be noticed by me.

He noses my arm and a glass of red wine spills over the arm of the $900 couch my wife bought last summer. I scream at him and he moves with the alacrity of a two-year-old and sits in the corner, facing away, pretending that nothing happened and everything is all right. If you look at a corner long enough and ignore everything behind you, everything will be all right.

Dogs are masters of self-deception.

Chubby is fourteen years old, graying at the muzzle, gimpy in the hips. What's a $900 couch between a couple of old friends? Increasingly old friends, as we find every morning when we groan and rise from our couches to go forth into the morning light and seek game birds.

Chubby is third in the dynasty that began with Guff, gravitated to Pepper, then to Chubby and Dacques, now is incumbent on Flick and Pucques and Tess's three kids, Missy, Scruff, and Jay. Four generations. If dogs were people, that might span nearly the history of the country.

But they aren't. They are born, they live, and they die with what seems the depressingly short life of a mayfly.

"You know you're gonna lose them when you get them," is the old saying about getting a dog. Maybe not. I'm sixty-five and if I get a puppy tomorrow he might outlast me.

But he might not. He might join the others on the gravesite across the lake and up the hill. Chubby has been with me a sixth of my life and it seems forever.

I remember him muzzle-deep in the pond as a chunky puppy. He was the first to take to the water and today he swims endless figure eights with the unrequited dream of catching a bluegill. He knows they swim beneath and around him, but he can't quite catch one.

His faith is boundless; if all Christians were as faithful, heaven would be overpopulated. Nothing discourages Chubby during the summer. He swims and swims and only reluctantly leaves his bluegill friends when it's time to go to the kennel. I think they consider him the bluegill god, for they swarm around him as if in divine adoration, not realizing he'd like to grab them in a death grip.

Although maybe he wouldn't. Chubby is as soft-mouthed as Michelle Pfeiffer teaching someone to French kiss (although not having had the pleasure of Pfeiffer teaching me the art of the kiss, I may be wrong there). Lightly winged quail have flown out of Chubby's mouth, and the bird he delivers is as dry as the Mohave, no slime of dog slobber desecrating its feathers.

I remember his first point the way you remember your kid's first words or first steps. We were in waist-high weeds in an old field and the other dogs had gone on ahead. Then I saw Chubby stopped as if he were thinking about something he'd forgotten to do, and I took a step forward and a glory of quail erupted from under his nose.

He has pointed countless birds since. He is a careful dog, not the best nose, not the widest ranger, but careful and penitent when he screws up. He cares.

When he was eleven, Chubby took a dive off a cliff, not a career move for an aging French Brittany. He was cruising the cliff top in pursuit of a quail covey that my son Andy and I had flushed. We found them at the base of the twenty-foot cliff and they came up in the proverbial cloud and we filled the ether with a haze of no. 7½ Winchester Hunter loads to moderate effect. A gunshot to Chubby is like a starter pistol and I saw him start sliding down the slope to the drop-off and shouted, "Chubby! No!"

But he was committed and he slid off the cliff and dropped twenty feet to what fortunately was fairly soft ground. I was certain he was seriously injured, but he didn't even whimper. He hit, bounced up, and began looking for birds. Chubby will run through brick walls when he is hunting, but he is the world's greatest wimp when he's not hunting. Pull a cocklebur and he will scream as if you were extracting his heart with nut picks. He can't stand pain if he's thinking about it. Once he hunted with a strong limp for a couple of weeks until we finally x-rayed him and the vet found a broken bone. Chubby then thumped around the house on the cast, like the mummy of the old horror movies, looking piteous and occasionally whining as if in agony.

He has reached an age when stuff hurts in the morning. Well, it does with me too. I wake in the chill dawn of a hunting shack and my knees send distress signals and my feet are eligible for federal disaster aid and the rest of me is even worse. But do I grumble about it?

Well, okay, I do . . . but not at the top of my voice. Chubby rises from his bed (the other bunk in the hunting shack) and stiffly totters across to my bunk in the dark of the predawn and screams in my face. Talk about a wake-up call. A dog screaming in the night is more traumatic than Howard Stern interviewing Michael Jackson.

Chubby invented his agonized scream when he was a puppy. He was in apparent distress (possibly because of something he ate) and we poked and prodded to see what was the matter. Any other dog would stoically endure it, but Chubby screamed and we were sure he had life-threatening internal injuries. Every touch, no matter how light, brought agonized howls. We rushed him to the vet, who examined him thoroughly and said, "I think this dog is a hypochondriac." And so it has proved.

I've wanted to write a tribute to Chubby for a long time. He's a special dog. Everyone has a dog they think is special, and to me a special dog is one that makes a difference in your life. Doesn't mean he's a perfect bird dog, nor that he is more intelligent than your children, nor more cuddly than your mate; it means he (or she) is . . . well, special.

Chubby is not the best bird dog in the kennel, but he's the smartest. "He knows everything I say," I tell my wife, who looks at me and slowly shakes her head. Chubby is a caring dog. He wants to make things right. Even when he makes them wrong. That's why he nuzzled my hand and tipped the red wine over the new couch.

He wasn't being devilish; he just wanted to remind me that he cared for me and that he was there if I wanted to love him and get loved in return. And he felt worse about staining the couch than I did. Dogs rarely if ever think of the consequences of their actions, but Chubby is quick to realize them.

Chubby did not feel worse, however, than my wife did.

I once was sick on a hunting trip with Chubby, the kind of malaise where you feel no one loves you and you're probably going to die a thousand miles from home. I lay down to go to my eternal reward (doubtless in a downward direction) and called Chubby. He leaped on the couch with me and nestled down by my head and went to sleep, his rhythmic breathing as soothing as a binkie to a colicky infant. Soon I drifted off too, and when I woke, Chubby was next to me, his fur as soft as baby's breath, and I felt fine. We hunted the next day and Chubby pointed birds for me. We were a team again. He had cured me.

It was as if an angel had laid hands on me. Yes, I know, that's sappy dog love and no real dog man would confess to such foolishness. But it has happened more than once. Maybe Chubby is not only the bluegill god; maybe he is my guardian angel.

I just know that when he grays even more and comes to the end of his hot little life I am going to be devastated, for he is part of me as surely as my vital organs.

"Chubby" is almost a demeaning name for such a presence in a person's life. He should be named King or Prince or, at the least, Lad. Chubby doesn't care what his name is. He's eternally sweet, eternally dedicated to two things: me and birds.

Could anyone ask more of a friend?

Chubby was born on the eve of Missouri's best quail season in twenty years. He was lucky to have as parents dogs whose blood swarms with Good Nose genes and a boss who is ape nuts over quail hunting. Any dog with that background couldn't help but be eternally happy, wriggly with the sheer joy of living.

The winter of Chubby's adolescence was no winter at all. A couple of scenic snowfalls quickly melted when the temperature shot into the fifties the same week. There were no below-zero temperatures, nor ice storms, so the birds that went into the winter came out of it in good shape, fat and sexy.

The formula was there for a whammo production year: good carryover of birds and a mild nesting season. I am always torn in the winter, for I am a fan of the north wind and the bitter storm. I like the feel of windblown snowflakes and the pristine tapestry a snowfall creates. But while snow and ice create a crystal palace for me, they vow death for the birds I hunt so lustfully.

"Do you ever think about the quail," I asked Chubby. "Out there in your snug little house that daddy built for you and that you have tried to reduce to toothpicks when gripped by boredom?"

Quail don't have insulated walls and clean, warm straw to de-fang the bite of the north wind. They're butt to butt under a red cedar tree, hoping that the sleet rattling off the shingled branches doesn't trickle through. They're feather-fluffed and stoic, and if cold weather were going to kill all the quail they wouldn't have been around when I first shouldered a single-shot Stevens 12-gauge that walloped my shoulder like an eight-pound maul. But there's a temperature point below which their fierce little engines just slow down and quit.

No problems that winter when Chubby was a porky little package of energy. Quail went into breeding season with yellow fat still ridged along their muscle bundles, little brown sexual time bombs. They started whistling love songs in early April, maybe ill-advised by the early spring, maybe just warming up their dormant pipes. A good sign, that piercing imperative from fence post and hay bale.

Of course, we always have to worry about heavy rains during the nesting period, especially in June when maybe 60 percent of the young birds will come off the nest, and again in August when the breeders that didn't make it the first time around will try again.

We could have a good hunting season if the first nest period is a success; we could have a season beyond a bird hunter's most intemperate whimsy if the August hatch proves a frothy topping to our annual dessert.

I told Chubby what a marvel it would be if *both* those nest periods were ideal. "My cuddly little French Brittany," I said. "You would throb like a tuning fork in the field, for you'd never be out of scent range of the little brown rockets. "Cummon, now, give me a kiss! What a time we're going to have!"

It had been twenty years since the previous superyear, back in the late 1960s when Chubby's grandpa wasn't a gleam in his mommy's eye because his mommy wasn't even born. Twenty years is a long time to wait for the brass ring to come around again.

It has been tough in the Midwest for us hard-core quail hunters. We had the worst winter on record back in '83 and game birds nose-dived. It was a sad, bitter time when coveys froze on the roost, their communal furnace gone clinkered and cold.

As I was crossing the Minnesota River in Minneapolis that year, temperature below zero in the daytime, I saw a rooster pheasant limping along the shoulder of Interstate 35, looking for something to eat. His magnificent coat of many colors was ragged and dispirited, as was he, facing another night of thirty below with nothing in his belly and his fires gone low.

He had plenty of company all across the Midwest. But, as if that had been winter's worst punch, the succeeding winters were increasingly mild. And as each mean time passed by without catastrophe, more breeding birds survived to fatten the fall population of quail and other Midwest game birds.

Quail are a troubled species nearly nationwide. Habitat loss is the prime factor, no doubt, but there are other factors in play. There are more predators today. There are more chemicals on the land. Habitat loss is a combination of many factors: urban sprawl, clean farming, ever larger fields, monoculture crops that leave no cover and no residue, conversion of legumes to fescue—the list is depressingly long.

But sometimes there is a felicitous congruence of good things, and quail make a temporary resurgence. The Conservation Reserve Program acreage has helped temporarily in many states (the ten-year set-aside contracts are good for quail for two or three years, then generally go to grass and become less valuable). Still, CRP is far better than no CRP, both for quail and for the health of the land.

Politicians are only marginally more adept at admitting environmental degradation than are most farmers, but it finally dawned on politicos and farmers alike that we are cropping the dirt to bedrock, raising beans and corn where bare ground is an engraved invitation to erosion to every passing raindrop or vagrant breeze.

By the time that banner year came around, Chubby had leaned out and gotten all growed-up. He was misnamed. I could feel his ribs and occasionally he was not first in the chow line.

As I said, Chubby was the first of the litter to hold a game bird in his mouth, trotting uncertainly here and there with worried eyes, flustered by the stirrings of his birthright. He sight-pointed a woodcock wing on the end of the fishing line and in other ways demonstrated that there was more than just cute beneath that glossy black-and-white hide. He learned the magic word "birrrrd!" even though he barely knew what it meant.

So I was waiting for this year much more than Chubby could know. All he knew was that the going was fun. He ran the fields and fencerows, tugged by subtle biological rhythms. What a thrill it would be when we found a corn stubble field where quail crouched and twittered with apprehension at the distant sound of a car door slamming and Guff's excited bark. What a thrill if we could find them and Chubby confronted his destiny.

I sat with my arm around Chubby the night before quail season opened and I said, "Let me tell you what's going to happen, little fat friend with the worried eyes. It will be cold and clear, an early winter, with frost on the ground at sunrise, no wind, breath hanging in the air like the meager ghosts of remembered hunts.

"You won't understand the portent of this moment, but Grandpa Guff will. He will leap and bark in a paroxysm of joy. Watch him, kid, because he knows where quail like to hang out and will snub the unproductive country. He high-grades, skims the cream off the cover and when he stops, splay-footed, narrow-eyed and whuffing, you'd better do the same, for there are nervous quail close by and puppies who fail to honor are puppies with sore butts.

"You won't know why I've whoa-ed you, but Guff will and he'll tremble slightly, his breath panting between slightly parted lips, like an obscene caller breathing heavily and suggestively. This is no rabbit, nor false point on last night's roost site, Chubby. This is real stuff and in a moment, the crisp air is going to be filled with a bewildering thunder of feathers and fuss.

"If all goes well, I'll kill one of those birds. If all goes beyond my wildest expectation, I'll kill two of them, but don't count on that. You'll hear the confusing roar of the covey rise and the almost simultaneous pound of two shots from the old L.C. Smith. How many quail has that old gun seen with its two hot eyes? How many would have flushed in front of it since 1910, when it was created by loving and long-dead hands?

"Then we get to look for the downed bird, Chubby. Guff would find it quickly, for he spots birds down as well as any dog, but I'll try to keep him back and let you poke around and if you're lucky and I can nudge you close, you may inhale the hot scent of the just-dead bird and something will snap in that little unformed brain and you'll freeze and quiver.

"All the threads of training, the months of patiently weaving the tapestry that will be you now are pulled and tucked and tied. The musty old woodcock wing you pointed instinctively and the imperative "Whoa!" and the walks afield when I demonstrated hand signals, gesticulating like a berserker and leaping into the brush as if pursued by cheetahs, all will have meaning from this moment forward."

I always wonder what happens inside a dog when it confronts bird stink for the first time. I wonder how a bird dog sorts out the scent of game birds from the myriad other odors that filter in and out of his pulsing nostrils. A dog who's never seen a pheasant instantly will point while ignoring blue jays, cardinals, any non-game bird.

Puppies point robins, but robins once were a game bird in the American South. Maybe there is some historic imperative that has been passed down, like canine folklore.

I hear talk of scent molecules and other jargon that fails to move me. A molecule is something Albert Einstein passed on his way to the atom and I'll bet neither he nor his dog smelled it even if it fell off a quail.

No, it's White Magic, a spell cast by Bird on dog and man, like the Good Witch of the North showering glitter dust over Dorothy. That's what it is, glitter dust in the air, stirred up by the anxious wings of quail, glitter dust in the nose of a bird dog. That's what puts the spell on him, makes him a bewitched dog.

And that's what makes me, the old guy with the tired lines around the eyes and the snow-capped thatch, become just for a while a princeling again, a young king with the future ahead and the sun just rising on tomorrow. Some don't understand the lure of the field and fencerow, the fun in following the bounding butt of a bird dog. But they have not known that moment when the Good Witch waves her magic wand and makes the little brown birds fill the crisp autumn air with glitter dust.

NINE

The Sweet Stink of Success

There are commercial tests to check the acuity of a bird dog's nose, but I have one that is never fail and low cost.

Most hunters are also anglers. So, catch a mess of fish, gut them, and bury the guts as deep as you can get a shovel in the ground. Allow a couple of days for them to ripen, loose the bird dogs, and see which ones come back odoriferous and oily.

Those are the choke-bored noses. But, given the bird dog's penchant for finding noxious substances in which to roll, the only difference between the sharpest-nosed one and the dullest-nosed is time—they'll all find and roll in gunk.

The same dog that can detect fish guts deeply buried will have stoned-nosed days in the field where he couldn't find a quail if it were stapled on the end of his muzzle. Why is that? You'd have to ask the dogs and they ain't tellin'.

Field experiments with radio-collared game birds prove that the average bird dog finds about 40 percent of the birds available. In other words, the guy who tells you Ol' Smoke will find 'em if they're there is likely to be wrong more than half the time. The best dogs (or the luckiest ones on the day they get tested) will find maybe two-thirds of the resident game birds.

But the dog who can't find any birds will have no trouble with those fish guts. I remember Guff having such a day, though I have long tried to forget those dread hours. They say every dog has his day, but when Guff had his, planets collided and stars rocked in the firmament. Saying this was a bad day was like saying an encounter with the guillotine is a "little owie."

You must understand, Guff was my pride, my gifted child, the kid who just spelled "anopheles" correctly in the spelling bee finals. Guff was not just any dog, you know, but a French Brittany with enough Gallic blue blood in his background to outdo the House of Burgoyne. His grandpa was a champ and his daddy was a champ. Most of his uncles and aunts won field and bench shows nationally and internationally. They looked on Westminster as "that silly little American show."

McGuffin was an ardent hunter who would come out of a sound sleep if someone murmured "birrrrd!" He was broad-chested with the typical butt-sprung gait of Brittanies. His dozen bird seasons included just about every game bird in North America—ruffed grouse, sharp-tailed grouse, woodcock, pheasant, quail. He worked them all, growing as reliable as Mr. Goodwrench.

Guff had a cute little freckled nose that made cute little freckled girls gush over him so I often took him to places where there were many cute freckled girls.

I would buy a sack of caramels every time we went north to the popple woods to hunt ruffed grouse and woodcock. Some were for me, some were for Guff, most for the family dentist who enjoys replacing my fillings and subsequently taking his own vacations in more southern climes.

The caramels kept our energy up as we stumbled through godforsaken swamp edges where the footing is somewhat like break dancing on a pool table covered with ball bearings.

Because Guff was first a quail dog, he had trouble with grouse. Since he only saw them once a year, he tended to forget they aren't just big quail who will sit right under a French Brit's black nose as if skewered there with a dirk.

Instead, grouse are stupid birds, brainless and indecisive. Anything foreign in their environment throws them into a mindless confusion that usually leads to movement—they either walk off or fly up in a tree, where they can be taken in what one of our hunters euphemistically refers to as "the preflight position." Or they fly off in a fluster of confusion that discombobulates hunters like no other game bird.

A French Brittany creeping forward like a roan cat definitely qualifies as "foreign," and Guff had trouble realizing that he must instantly freeze at the merest whiff of grouse stink, no matter the direction, that he must not try to locate that smell or make it grow stronger. He had trouble learning that a bird walking around on the ground is not necessarily crippled and will fly if you try to catch it.

So it was understandable that he had the occasional bad day. But this bad day was the Johnstown Flood compared to an overflowing toilet.

Guff started it by falling off his bed. He'd sneaked up on the overstuffed chair in the old cabin where we stay and, probably dreaming of cute little freckled ladies, rolled over and onto the floor with a thump that woke everyone up.

We all thrashed around in bed, grumbled a bit, and went back to troubled, interrupted sleep. God knows what Guff dreamed about, but no matter how wild his reverie, it couldn't have approached the reality that was fast approaching him.

I was expansive at breakfast, telling a disbelieving audience in the log cabin where we shuck civilization that I had reformed. "No more screaming at the dog," I said and they smirked. "No," I protested, "I mean it. Just not worth the hassle. Besides, the dogs have settled down and I just don't need to run them down and speak long and earnestly at them. We're both mature now." I smiled paternally at Guff. Me and my doggie, finding grouse, shooting them, a scene to warm the cold, revered shade of Burton Spiller.

I spoke the words and believed them. Ah, words with barbed wire wrapped around them, the toughest kind to digest when you have to eat them.

"Zen dog training," said one of the hunters. "I'll swallow that when I see it."

Ted and I walked the edge of a doghair popple stand that crowded a pasture. I searched the thick saplings in vain for the noble sight of my dog, descendant of champions, as he coursed the covert. Then a movement caught my eye, in the field beyond.

There was my noble dog snacking on a cow pie, his shoulder drooped and twitching, like Charles Laughton in *The Hunchback of Notre Dame*, ready to roll in what he didn't eat. It may come as a shock to new dog owners to think that their endearing companions would eagerly snack on bovine biscuits, but life with bird dogs is filled with such taut moments of unhappy discovery. My Zen calm went out the window and I roared ancient Anglo-Saxon while Ted tried to pretend he was hunting alone.

I lost it again after the third point Guff busted. Zen went the way of my resolve never to touch Scotch and water again, never to buy another shotgun, never to lie about my shooting. I laid curses on Guff that you couldn't cancel with an exorcism. I held him by the cheeks while I explained in dog language what I expected. Dog language is sheer, roaring filth that even the most inane creature comprehends.

Perhaps Guff pointed a grouse that day, but if so it was done while I wasn't with him. I do know that he busted at least a half dozen birds, most of which had been nailed by Ted's setter, Salty, until Guff came along like a derailed cattle car.

You can steal a man's children, corrupt his wife, ruin his business, or even insult his baseball team. But let your bird dog bust up a point that his bird dog has made and you've really ticked him off. Ted began to look at Guff as if he were head lice, then looked at me as if I were the head.

I muttered about "competition" and "doesn't realize you can't lean on grouse" and Ted muttered something about "take that dog's head off with a two-by-four."

Salty was becoming jittery, Ted was becoming . . . well, homicidal is the word that springs to mind. Fortunately, the sun took pity on me and started to go down.

We headed back to the cabin by the river. Guff, of course, had to assistant-drive, his face between us, panting a fog of recycled manure. Back in the cabin I regaled a bored audience with tales of Guff's misbehavior. "He was disgraceful," I said. "He made every mistake in the book and invented some new ones. He was terrible." As I spoke, Dave Mackey's face grew alarmed and I thought it was with horrified sympathy. It wasn't.

"Watch out!" Mackey exclaimed. "He's sick!"

Guff threw up on the carpet behind me, a slurry of awfulness that took an hour to clean. Clearly this was a dog beset by devils, a victim of black magic or a curse. The red gods were playing dodgeball with my dog and me.

Guff looked at me with sick apology and suddenly I felt sorry for the little guy and tried to consider the big picture. After all, for every bad day, he'd given me so many good ones. For every point he'd busted, he'd made a dozen good ones in the past.

I tried to correlate the day's experience in human terms, and the television set helped me. The St. Louis Cardinals had just won their way into a tie with the San Francisco Giants behind shutout pitching by ace John Tudor. Tudor had pitched like a Little League dropout his previous game; couldn't do anything right.

Obviously, even the best have their off days.

So I relented and petted the little dog and he sighed heavily and pouted off to a corner to lie atop Dave Mackey's hunting pants, which were draped over his box of ammo and gun cleaning gear.

We watched *The Equalizer,* whose methods of correction (throw them through brick walls, etc.) were close to what I'd considered all day long for Guff.

Dave picked his pants up the next morning and they were dripping with WD-40. Guff had laid on the nozzle of the full spray can and emptied it.

His bad day was complete.

Hold a game bird up to your nose sometime. Aside from a slight musty, feathery scent, you won't smell anything. You couldn't find a game bird by scent on the best day you ever had.

But a dog can on its worst day because its nose is so far superior to that of a human. The use of dogs to sniff out contraband is widespread and well established. Dope- and bomb-sniffing dogs are a staple of many a law enforcement agency.

Even the wildlife agencies have gotten into dog cops. Florida's Game and Freshwater Fish Commission was the first outdoor agency to be certified by the U.S. Police Canine Association and has been a training ground for other K–9 programs. Both Indiana and South Carolina sent officers to train with the Florida canine cops.

Most use the dogs as sniffers, not for enforcement. And most are Labradors, but Florida has a couple of Chesapeakes and one German shorthair.

The faith that people have in the accuracy of a dog's nose is demonstrated by an incident in Indiana. Wildlife officer Scott Wilson recalled a case where agents saw a poacher at a distance, hunting out of season with a muzzleloader. But when the poacher came out of the woods, he was carrying a stick and, in common with poachers everywhere, claimed he didn't know anything about a gun, hadn't done anything wrong.

Wilson opened the car door for the dog and the poacher sighed and said resignedly, "Never mind—the dog will find it anyway," and led them to the gun he'd ditched.

Other wildlife dogs have found lost hunters and kids or smelled out illegal game. But the mystery of how dogs do what they do with their noses is just that—a mystery. And until dogs learn to talk, it will never be solved.

Most hunters think they know about scenting conditions. They nod knowledgeably and opine, "Yep, it's about perfect today—little frost on the ground, little breeze, warm sun. Oughta be able to find birds a half mile away." I've even seen charts compiled by outdoor writers on scenting conditions, good and bad.

Good is high humidity, maybe wet snow, temperature between thirty and forty degrees . . . the list goes on. Bad conditions are low humidity, high winds, and so forth. Okay, I watched a shorthair point chukar partridges flawlessly all day. It was in the typically arid habitat cherished by chukars and the scenting conditions, according to the chart, were all wrong. Apparently the dog hadn't learned to read.

Scenting is subject to so many variables that no one can predict it with any certainty. Convection, wind direction and speed, the terrain, amount of vegetation, and many other factors all come into play in complex ways that can either facilitate or frustrate the dog.

A human sheds about 40,000 cells every minute (kind of frightening, isn't it). Some of them are lighter than air and float in the breeze. Others fall to earth and become ground scent. Because of its smaller size, a game bird floats fewer cells, but they're there. Even an immobile bird or covey is lofting lighter-than-air scent particles which, if the wind and all those other variables are right, will betray the game to the dog.

A dog is supposed to have anywhere from 100 million to 230 million scent cells in its nose (I have no idea who counted them). This compared to about 5 million in a human.

Whatever the equation of human versus dog scent cells, there's no doubt the dog is almost infinitely superior. My father earned a living selling perfume oils and his nose literally was his livelihood. But the best day he ever had, scentwise, he couldn't compete with the most stone-nosed dog. The dog has olfactory weapons both inside and outside its nose. Next time Ol' Sport sticks a wet nose into forbidden territory, causing you to leap like an impala, shriek and cuss but don't blame him, at least for the cold nose.

The moisture on a dog's nose traps scent molecules and dissolves them for identification. Likewise, the dog's wet tongue helps trap airborne scent. Some maintain that a bird dog can wind-scent game birds a quarter mile away. Perhaps, although I can't say that I've ever seen it.

No aroma, including that of game birds, is as enticing to male dogs as that of a bitch in heat. As I write we have a female in heat and six males in the kennel, all of whom are hoarse from barking their love. They certainly can find the spot where Missy urinated. Release them from the kennel and it looks like either a puck drop in hockey or a crap game—six dogs clustered around a spot the size of a half-dollar.

If a dog could wind at a quarter mile, I would think the several neighbor dogs, all of whom live closer than that, would be hanging around our backdoor like encyclopedia salesmen. But I haven't seen any of them. They haven't gotten the wind-borne message.

I'm dubious about the claims of hunters who say their dog can wind-scent birds way out there, just as I am dubious about those who claim that if any birds are in the area their dog will find them. That latter claim has been proved (by electronic collar) to be false. I suspect if anyone is running distance-scenting experiments, they're finding a dog's nose is less than advertised.

Still, the estimate of five hundred times better dog versus man nose probably isn't far off. It's fascinating to me to speculate on why a dog will not react to something really noxious (or will react diametrically opposite of what I would). You'd think a dog, confronted with a reeking pile of guts that's almost overwhelming to a human, would keel over when blasted with five hundred times what the human gets.

Obviously the dog processes scent far differently than we do. Albert Payson Terhune, the famous collie writer, claimed his collies were offended by cigarette smoke. I don't know if that was because they really were or because Terhune was offended by cigarette smoke (his reportage credited his collies with traits more like saintly humans than dogs).

Dogs seem to take scent—good or bad—in stride. Their value judgments apparently rest on "good for me" or "not interesting for me," rather than simply "good" or "bad." I've seen dogs go wary around skunks, porcupines, and snakes, but I don't think that reaction was solely because of scent—it probably was some atavistic instinct that triggered a general alarm.

Larry Myers, a professor of veterinary medicine at Auburn University, is the nation's leading noseologist (I made that up, by the way). He has done more research on dog scenting than anyone.

I asked him why, if a dog's nose is so sensitive to odor, the dog doesn't just fall over stunned when assaulted by stinks that offend humans. He says CS gas, a kind of tear gas that will incapacitate a human, has no effect on a dog.

I have read that while bird dogs react instinctively to some game birds, they must be trained to work others. I'm not convinced. I've seen my dogs key on an entirely new game bird while ignoring the indigenous non-game ones. A friend wrote that his shorthair ignored woodcock until it realized the master wanted them hunted. Every one of my dogs has worked woodcock on first contact, so my friend's experience and mine are completely opposite.

You could theorize that game birds, being mostly genetically related, have a common scent factor, but woodcock,
for example, are not related to the wild chicken family
(grouse, quail, pheasants). It's frustrating not to be able to
ask the dog what's going on with its nose and brain (or at
least ask and get an answer).

How does a dog know which way a trailed creature
went? Perhaps the scent is slightly stronger in one direction
than another. Again, some say the dog cannot discriminate
if it cuts a trail, but I think it does—without any proof except empirical. A dog hot on the trail of a running pheasant will ignore cross trails and stay with the target bird.
Perhaps that's because each bird has a distinctive scent or
because the trailed bird has the tiniest bit hotter scent.

Once I saw Guff go on point, but he was not locked
down and I figured he had a rabbit. You get to know your
dogs and read when they're playing beagle or are really serious. His body language was beaglese. "Go on, Guff!" I
commanded in some irritation. A friend whom I wanted to
impress was hunting with me for the first time and I didn't
want him to see my treasured bird dog point a rabbit or,
God forbid, chase it. Guff stayed on point but moved his
head in confusion. "Geez, get serious," I grumbled and
stepped in front of him. And two coveys of quail, about
twenty yards apart, flushed left and right. He had been almost exactly midway between them.

There is no meaningful way you can apologize to a dog.
They don't understand "I'm sorry," and they don't really
care. We're the only one of the pair that feels bad (or at
least should).

Bird dogs are rarely wrong and a good rule of thumb is to believe the dog. The times when the dog is messing with possums or rabbits or turtles are few; the times when it is confronted with a genuine puzzle are many. It may be a wild turkey. My dogs have pointed many in cover so thin you'd swear it couldn't hide a field mouse. The awesome flush is breathtaking for dog and man alike.

If it weren't for the nose, we might as well leave the dog at home, unless we're strapped for something to yell at. We can recognize good cover as easily as a dog can and, while the dog can cover far more ground than we can, we can high grade what we see. But we can't smell those birds that might be huddled in the thicket, waiting for us to pass by.

Any pheasant hunter has seen his dogs catch birds that burrowed into thick vegetation and couldn't get airborne. There have been days when the dog's score was higher than mine. Those birds would have been as safe as Fort Knox gold had the dog not caught their scent.

Sometimes I hold Scruffy cheek to cheek and watch his nose ever flexing and I wonder, *What are you seeing that I'm not? What myriad scents are flowing in a jumble through those two nostrils and somehow getting sorted out into usable information?*

It is a miracle of nature every bit as astonishing as any and certainly more mysterious because there's no way to study it, no visible evidence of what is happening.

So we explain dog-scenting with molecules and other wise-sounding scientific jargon. I prefer to believe it's White Magic.

TEN

Travels with Charley's Peers

John Steinbeck wrote a book about a trek around the country with a poodle named Charley. While Steinbeck is among my favorite authors, his choice of a poodle as a traveling companion makes me wonder. Not that there's anything wrong with poodles, aside from the fact that they're poodles, but when a Brittany is available, why take a poodle on a trip?

Although I have to admit poodles possibly are marginally smarter than my Brittanies, they don't point birds and they're too damn curly. Stanley Coren's fine book *The Intelligence of Dogs* (Macmillan, 1994) ranks dogs according to working intelligence, and he ranks the border collie tops, followed by the poodle. The German shepherd is third and the golden retriever (the first hunting dog) is fourth.

My cherished Brittanies are ranked nineteenth, far ahead of Gordon setters (tied for 34th), English setters

(37th), and pointers (43d). But they are well behind the Lab at seventh, and slightly behind their upland confreres, the springers at thirteenth, German shorthair at seventeenth, and English cocker at eighteenth. Wouldn't trade my Brits for any of those show-off smarty pants, although there are times on the road when I'd trade them for a fastidious cat.

I try to stay in motels with a back entrance through which I can sneak the dogs for a night of comfort, instead of being cramped in their frigid kennels in the back of the truck. But even at their seediest, motels were not created for bird dogs. You'll see no signs reading "Super Eight Kennel" or "Marriott Menagerie."

But my Brittanies remain unconvinced. Given a choice of sleeping in prickly straw in a Porta Kennel in the back of a dirty pickup truck with the temperature in single digits . . . or going inside with The People and doing what people do there (brag on shooting prowess, complain about aching body parts, and watch the weather forecast on television), what do you, Noble Scruffy, do?

The motel has a big soft bed with no straw and a huge drinking bowl that's all white and far nicer than the usual plastic bucket (if daddy remembers to lift the lid). And you get to sleep with daddy.

Okay, pointer men are gagging at the thought of dogs sleeping with them. Except when we are on the road, our dogs spend their nights in doghouses, grumbling at kennel mates and sighing over the memory of the rare times when they get to sleep with me.

A dry, bur-free dog makes a good sleep toy. There's something comforting about a dog nestled close. Some of us aren't that far from our nursery days (emotionally speaking, not geriatrically). Linus has his blanket; I have my Brittany.

A friend told me the following apocryphal story. Seems a dog owner asked if his dog would be welcome in his motel room and received the following reply: "I've been operating this motel for many years. In all that time I've never had a dog steal towels, bedclothes, silverware, or pictures off the wall. I've never had to evict a dog in the middle of the night for being drunk and disorderly and I've never had a dog run out on a motel bill.

"Yes, your dog is welcome, and if your dog will vouch for you, you're welcome too."

On the other hand, how many times do people relieve themselves on the carpet at 2 a.m.?

Most motel nights are quiet, with dogs and hunters too worn out to get into trouble. But there are exceptions that stud my memory like black holes into which the stars fall and implode.

Once I let four dogs into a motel hallway and they raced toward my room, making no more noise than a bison stampede. Halfway there they veered into an open doorway (as smart as Brits are, they haven't learned to read room numbers) and jostled into the bathroom to drink from the toilet.

A stranger was talking on the phone. He didn't stop, but looked at me the way a dowager looks at vomit on her Persian rug. The dogs drank noisily and I hissed, "Come!"

to which they paid no attention. They were thirsty and I wasn't screaming at them the way I do when I'm really upset, so they figured I wasn't serious.

I dragged them one by one to my room, which meant four trips into the stranger's bathroom. He continued to talk on the phone, but his eyes never left me and I slunk out with the last dog, leaving behind an empty toilet bowl and a slimy trail of dog slobber.

Once I led two dogs down a Super Eight corridor late at night. The clerk had eyed me suspiciously when I checked in and noticed a prominent No Pets sign at the desk.

I was almost to the room, the dogs skulking behind me, when a burly man who epitomized a motel security guard suddenly appeared and squinted at me, then the dogs. It was snowing outside and bitterly cold and I was exhausted. I really didn't want to be thrown out of the motel.

I gulped and gave him a tentative smile. He looked again at me, then at the dogs.

"Nice dogs," he said.

Motels, dogs, and I began our rocky relationship years ago. The first pheasant I ever shot was lolling on the tail-gate of my station wagon as I checked in. When I came back, the rooster had vanished and the motel owner's immense Labrador was wagging his tail, with a telltale feather caught at the corner of his mouth. I cleaned quail in the sink that night and later was told the feathers clogged the drain and flooded the room. It's enough to make you believe in divine retribution.

Most dogs realize they are sub rosa in a motel and will keep quiet, but my longtime best friend Guff always announced the dawn with one sharp bark that echoed through the motel like cannon fire. He couldn't help it. He was so excited to greet another day that it just erupted, like Mount St. Helens.

Other dog eruptions are less agreeable, especially to the maid. In a South Dakota restaurant I asked the waitress if the cook might have a little bit of meat juice to entice tired dogs into eating dry dog food.

She brought a huge cup, brimming with *jus de boeuf*. Anyone with half a brain would suspect that too much of that rich brew would resonate through a dog's digestive system like a runaway subway train rocketing through the tunnel. But I slopped it on the food until it was gone and the four dogs ate as if they hadn't seen food for a week.

I was awakened in the pit of the night by the redolent aroma of dog deposits. There were three of them, neatly in line with the foot of my bed. Only Dutch among the four Brittanies had managed to retain what she'd eaten.

My lower back was spasming from the tough day's hunt, and bending over to scoop up dog excrement involved several kinds of agony. Lacking a pooper scooper, I used the motel ice bucket. You might want to think about that the next time you settle in for a cool drink in a motel room.

But at least I didn't stick my foot in something nasty in the dark of the night. My hunting buddy Spence Turner once rose to attend to nature's imperative, and his bare foot squished through a sludge of vomit, left there by a setter with an upset stomach.

"She threw up somebody's shorts!" Spence roared when he turned on the light. I never examined the evidence—didn't want to—and they weren't my shorts, so I went back to sleep. The shorts were red and no one admitted to owning them, so their source remains a mystery and we still talk about it.

Just not to Spence.

My sweet little female, Tess, was as quiet as the proverbial mouse so long as I was in the room with her. She would not stir the entire night. But let me leave the room and she became a frenzy of teeth.

Once I was hunting with a meticulous person who always wore pajamas. He would arrange them carefully each morning on his pillow, ready for the next night's sleep.

I left Tess and two other dogs in the room while I field-dressed several quail. Motel dumpsters are convenient for disposing of bird guts, though the management is less enchanted by this option than I am.

I was gone about five minutes. When I opened the door, Tess, breathing heavily, had just finished turning my hunting partner's pajamas into rags. She was the epitome of the unattended dog. Leaving a bird dog alone anywhere but in a stainless steel–lined room is asking for disaster.

A friend once left a Labrador alone in a motel room while he went to dine. He actually thought of the potential for trouble and shut the Lab in the tile-and-porcelain bathroom, figuring even a determined retriever couldn't do much damage in a ceramic room.

But when he returned and opened the motel door, a wall of water engulfed him. The Lab had gotten in the bathtub, stomped the drain plug in, and somehow managed to turn the water on. The ecstatic Lab greeted his master with a grin and a happy tail. Few motel dogs are furnished with their own swimming pool.

My son-in-law, Ron deValk, has great potential as a dog-in-the-motel man. On a pheasant hunt, he let our four dogs into the room and shut the door. Shortly there was a knock and a voice growled, "You can't have those dogs in there!"

"So, what happened?" I asked.

Ron shrugged. "I just ignored him and he went away."

My most memorable dog-in-the-motel experience was on New Year's Eve in north Missouri. I celebrated the end of the old year with an exhausting quail hunt and was in bed asleep long before the new year came 'round.

I like to sleep cool, so I spun the thermostat all the way over and snuggled into the blankets. Guff and Chubby picked spots on the carpet.

In the middle of the night I woke with Guff panting hard in my face. His breath was less than springlike. The room was unbearably hot. I hadn't turned the thermostat off; I'd turned it all the way up. It was about ninety-five degrees.

I sighed and turned the heat down, then decided to drain the dogs, both of whom were hopping from one leg to the other ("turning yellow" as Andy says). I pulled on a pair of pants, but no shirt or shoes, and stepped into the crisp night.

The stars glittered and my breath eddied in the icy air. But the room had functioned like a sauna. I'd stored enough heat that the winter air felt balmy . . . for a few seconds.

Chubby is kin to a camel. He can drink endlessly, go for what seems like days without a bathroom break, then drain endlessly. He chose the motel owner's plastic Santa Claus as his target and began to hose it, on and on, as I got colder and colder. I shifted from one bare foot to the other, felt my toes going numb. I beat my arms and blew on my hands.

"Come on, Chubby, for God's sake!" I hissed at the dog, who still stood, leg upraised, spraying jolly St. Nick.

Finally as I was nearing hypothermia, Chubby ran dry and I turned gratefully to the motel door . . . and found that it had snapped shut. The keys, of course, were inside on the nightstand.

The answer to potential motel damage is, of course, to invest an amount of money sufficient to finance a small-scale nuclear war in a recreational vehicle. Traveling with bird dogs in a recreational vehicle is tolerable only if you compare it with traveling through deep space while an alien being prowls through the plumbing.

I once took my dogs to Minnesota for a grouse hunt in a Winnebago Itasca Sundancer (an almost biblical lineage). The vehicle was both brand-new and borrowed. Loaning a glistening Winnebago to a bird hunter is like the television commercial in which they stuff a $40,000 Mercedes with crash dummies and run it into a concrete abutment.

Ah, sharing a hunting trip with Dacques and Chubby, the Brittany Brothers. We followed the lure of the open road in a mobile hunting shack. You could have more fun break dancing with cougars.

When first I thought of the idea, it sounded fine, like Steinbeck traveling the country with Charley, his poodle. We'd experience on-the-road adventures together and I would write about them and maybe win a Pulitzer.

The first fine adventure was the vomit on the carpet. Eagerly I checked past Pulitzer awards and found none ever had been granted for writing on dog vomit. Already I was deep in research on an unplumbed subject. Things were looking up!

After ten days on the road with two bird dogs, I was thinking booby prize, not Pulitzer. By then the Dogabago made a boar's nest look like Miss Sally's Tearoom. Dogs were not intended for an RV. No matter how clean the dog is at the beginning of the day, he will be a shivering, muddy, tattered mess after several hours of slogging through Minnesota swamp edges.

I parked in a sandy spot and both the dogs and I tracked in damp sand after each dewfall. I spent precious hunting moments brushing ineffectually at little dunes that had gathered under the seats and against the walls.

There is no option: either keep the RV clean by keeping it dog-free or, if you're on a bird hunting trip, load up the dogs and surrender to filth.

Of course, you can protect the RV by towing a dog trailer. But I'm leery of trailers, having managed to back more than one into something large and unyielding. I don't want to squash Dacques and Chubby between a rock and a hard place. Besides, a friend towing a dog trailer ran

into a violent winter storm and wound up with the dogs in
the RV while he towed the empty trailer behind, so he
didn't gain much.

The smell of dogs filled the air in the Dogabago, not to
mention the upholstery, with the reek of eau de mutt. It
was a mobile kennel and I had been demoted from kennel
master to kennel mate.

There were other distractions as well. Dogs are fond of
licking themselves (nevermind where) in the pit of the
night, and the metronomic slurping is enough to incite
murder.

The outrages went on night and day. At the end of
each day's hunt, the Dogabago suffered a little bit more.
Next time you're at an RV show, look around the interior
of the most luxurious vehicle. Then close your eyes and
imagine a muddy dog, slobbering from heat as it leaps into
the seats and bounds across the carpeting, and then begins
to chew out and spit cockleburs.

Dacques and Chubby are brothers. As the father of
brothers, I know that sibling rivalry is never more than a
growl away. Just as J.B. and Eddie grew up growling at each
other over the human equivalent of bones, so have the
Brittany Brothers.

If Chubby has it, Dacques wants it and vice versa.
Chubby could be gnawing at a road-killed vulture and
Dacques would growl that he wanted it, even as he
gagged.

The dogs argued about everything. If I put down two
bowls of water, they crowded at one, growling. Inevitably,
one stepped in the other bowl, slopping it on the carpet.

When dogs are present, any stainable substance is as sure to be spilled on the RV carpet as the sun is to come up the next morning. Dogs do not realize that a $42,000 Winnebago is different from a hay wagon. A rusted-out pickup held together by a slime of dried dog food and old slobber is the same to them as an RV only affordable to those whose mail largely consists of dividend checks from the Fortune 500.

Plan on returning the RV to its rightful owner with carpeting that looks as if it last was used to swab out a stable. The best flooring for a Dogabago is stainless steel. I tried to minimize the damage by shoving a Porta Pet kennel under the table. It's difficult to eat when a dog is licking your feet, but at least the dog can't defile the bed.

Dogs are creatures of conditioning. They learn by repetition. So, from many years on the road, Dacques and Chubby have learned that when we're on the road they get to sleep with me. People who own pointers will not understand the concept of sleeping with a dog. Sleeping with a pointer would be like sleeping with a concrete abutment.

But I grow lonesome on the road and long for a warm, comforting back to nestle against. Most dogs are restless and can't learn to lie properly (i.e., oriented as you are, not butt to face).

The dog should not kick or stir in the night. It must stretch out at the proper angle, providing both space and warmth. It must not shuffle, whuffle, or snore. And licking of intimate parts is strictly forbidden.

Dacques and Chubby have compromised. Chubby is my cheek dog and Dacques my foot dog. Dacques doesn't like that, but the master has spoken in those four-letter phrases that he is fond of and that bird dogs understand.

Dacques is a hard dog, built to demolish brick walls. He is a canine version of Arnold Schwarzenegger. Chubby, on the other hand, is fleecy, like a sleep toy. He plops into exactly the right spot, stirs just a bit to get comfortable, then is out for the night. Sometimes if I wake with midnight malaise, I hear him breathing softly, content in his easy dreams, and I relax.

A Winnebago or its equivalent is the ultimate hunting shack. It has all the amenities and you can move it around from hunting field to hunting field. There is a potty, with a shower (the shower head is right over the potty, meaning that if you want, you can take care of many necessary chores at the same time). The kitchenette is compact. In a Dogabago that means you can fall over a dog by taking a step in any direction.

People forget that an RV is not a home. You don't stumble down the hall to the bathroom; you pivot out of bed, like Michael Jordan going for a lay-up. By the time you're upright, you're also in the cubicle.

My Dogabago had a $200 coffeemaker option, which indicates some people cherish coffee more than I do. I heated water and made instant coffee that tasted like drain-trap residue, but at 5 a.m. it jump-started my vital functions.

If I can get myself in the mind-set of a Brittany, which isn't difficult since I am as elemental as rock, I can accept their transgressions and revel in the joy of their company. While I agonize over the deterioration of the Dogabago, I would be in worse pain without the dogs.

The dogs don't give a damn if they're in Vermont or California as long as they are with me and we are going somewhere, anywhere. We could be headed for the vet and they would be leaping around, exclaiming, "Oh, boy! Gee whiz! We're gonna go! We're gonna go!"

That attitude changes dramatically when they glimpse the vet clinic sign. Dogs may not be able to read, but they certainly know the shape and form of *that* sign.

After a long day in the bird fields, it is a great comfort to come back to the shack-on-wheels, tired to the bone, cold, scratched, and abused, and shut the door on the outdoors, flip on the radio to nice music and settle back in Mr. Winnebago's plush upholstery.

The dogs find a comfortable spot (not on the bed until they shed dirt and burs) and drift off to twitchy dog dreams.

The coffeepot is simmering quietly and the sun is a last promise on the horizon. It is an election year and the radio is shrill with the silly fulminations, recriminations, and evasions of politicians. They're as two-dimensional as Bugs Bunny, but far less entertaining.

Chubby is underfoot. This night I won't let him on the bed because in addition to swamp edge scruff, I treated a scrape with a gooey antiseptic that I don't want on the bedclothes. Chubby pouts for a while, then sneaks under the privacy screen into the driver's seat where he watches the sunset and the mallards trading up and down the river.

Dacques, who is slightly more resigned to being a dog, is in the kennel under my feet. The heat kicks on and steam rises from my coffee.

Tomorrow we'll be heading back to the grouse woods, a tangle of popple sprouts and alder sprawls, another day of mud and feathers to visit on the Dogabago.

But for tonight we're cozy in our portable hunting shack, just a boy and his dogs.

ELEVEN

Old Friends

In modern times, the greatest natural resource for most hunters is a place to hunt.

As we've urbanized, we've lost our ties to the country. My father moved to Chicago from a hard-rock Missouri farm in the 1920s, but he always had a home place to return to.

That home place was sold a few years ago. All of my father's generation are dead; their sons and daughters in their sixties and seventies. And *none*, not one of those children from a big family, now farms. Every single one lives in a city, as do their children.

Someone I don't know now owns my father's home place. He outbid a neighbor I grew up with and he didn't look agreeable to letting others hunt the old place, so I didn't ask.

So, the farm kid and his kids and their kids have lost a natural resource and are in danger of losing their will to hunt. After all, hunting is not an internal human desire, like hunger or thirst. It's a deeply ingrained tradition and a great pleasure, but like most pleasures if we don't exercise it, we lose interest.

Even those with a lingering desire to hunt must have a place to go. Public land is the solution for many, but there is no way in most parts of the country that public land can satisfy with enough game. My home, Missouri, has a half million acres of Conservation Department land and a half million or so hunters. A good upland wildlife area will see a procession of quail hunters every weekend and holiday—people almost always trying to escape city life and find something lost two generations ago and possibly don't even realize they miss. They only know there's something that must be better than endless televised football games, golf, and bowling.

Those of us who live in rural areas but aren't fortunate enough to own our hunting grounds depend on the generosity of others when we hunt private land. I hunt often with Dave Mackey, a Natural Resources Conservation Service district conservationist who, by the nature of his job, has access to much rural land in his county. He's gregarious and understands the delicate nature of landowner/sportsman relations. He carefully cultivates landowner friends, partly because he is a hunter and wants access but mostly because he is a landowner himself and understands their problems . . . and also because he likes and admires the landowners whose land he hunts on.

He is a treasure for me, first as a friend and mentor but also as a source of bountiful places to hunt. Dave would be my friend regardless. We enjoy each other's company. We solve world problems, kid each other, and discuss the rough spots in our lives. We are friends.

The area where I live mostly is fescue pasture, and quail are a thin commodity. I can't offer Dave a blue ribbon hunt where I live because they don't exist. He has better fishing and hunting where he lives; there's no reason to struggle with my meager potential.

So, what can I do for Dave as thanks for sharing what is a quail hunter's most priceless natural resource, his hunting land? I wish I knew. Any tokens are better than no tokens, but are they enough? Put it this way: if you hunt at a preserve or shooting club, you'll pay at least $100/day. If you lease land, say 1,000 acres (which for a party of four quail hunters isn't too much), you'll pay $10 or more/acre annually. Either way, bird hunting involves hundreds, even thousands of dollars if you have to buy it . . . and my friend is giving it to me for nothing.

There are some weighty questions here. What is friendship and how do you measure it? Do you reduce it to dollars and cents and try to balance it, like a corporate account ledger? Does it jeopardize a friendship to think who owes whom and how much? Is there a time when the "have" friend begins to think of the "have-not" friend as a freeloader? Or, conversely, should the "have-not" friend call a halt and say, "I've freeloaded on you long enough and I just can't do it anymore."

Maybe I'm making too much of it. I talked with my hunting buddy, Spence Turner, about this. Spence has shared farms with me for more than thirty years. He has better places to hunt than I do. But I've invited him on hunting trips that I arranged, and I've introduced him to a couple of other friends on whose land we've hunted for years. Still—am I behind on my debt? Or is there even a debt?

Spence's answer: "Don't worry about it."

Can't help it. I do worry about not carrying my share of the load, whatever the situation. Some years back, there was a person I considered a friend who proved to be all take and no give. He made promises he didn't keep and he didn't pay some of the freight when we were cost-sharing on hunting trips. He may have been careless, but it went on too long and it soured our relationship and we aren't friends anymore.

I also have been the "taker," the one who hunts on others, even getting free bed and board in the process, but unable to reciprocate. I do what I can: give subscriptions to *Gun Dog* magazine or bring token gifts or pick up the occasional meal tab. But I can never give Dave or Spence or any other friend what they give me, which is a blue ribbon place to hunt.

That's the sticking point. One fellow I know measures friendship on a quid pro quo basis. "I can't fish with a man, hunt with a man, or even have lunch without thinking about how I can return the favor in the same way," he says.

I replied, "Maybe I'm looking at this the wrong way, but I don't think friendship is a 'quid pro quo' arrangement. I don't do anything for a friend because I figure I owe him anything or that it's my turn. I do it because I like the friend and want to share something of mine with that person. What I share more than anything is time. If people really are friends, that's the most important gift they can give each other."

I really believe that if I were rich in hunting spots, I would welcome my friends to them and feel good when they had good hunts and that would be reward enough. I would not, I think, even consider that they then would owe me something.

That's what I believe . . . but since I don't have those areas, I don't know if the reality would be different than the perception. Things have a way of changing when it comes time to pay the bill.

After wrestling the question in my mind for years, I still don't know if my feelings are right or not. My quid pro quo friend is a lawyer. "When you spend as many years as I have in striking balances, it is impossible to perceive of any other system of human interchange," he said. "Quite frankly, nothing else works where I live. In every case, something must be given for everything gotten. It becomes a way of life and for the most part is how things are done. 'There is no free lunch' is more than a saying, at least in my world."

To me, that's a constipated and sour view of friendship . . . but I may be wrong and that's what has caused me to lose sleep and to question my motives and my whole concept of friendship. It's not the kind of thing you can ask a friend: "Tell me honestly, do you think I've taken advantage of you for the last twenty-five years?"

What is he going to say? "Yeah, you have, you jerk! Get out of my life!"

Not likely.

Or, "No. I like to have you visit and we always have fun together."

Chances are that's what he'd say . . . but once the niggling doubt is there, you wonder if he really means it. I wish I knew what it takes to cement a real friendship. Or I wish I could take Spence's advice and just not worry about it.

Everyone has buddy stories and it's a commonality that so many of them involve the less appealing facts of life: the elimination of bodily waste. I recall Bill Bennett, my longtime friend from St. Joseph, announcing the need to relieve himself outside our duck blind.

He squished across the marshy ground and proceeded to his toilette. In the middle of it a gang of mallards made a sudden appearance and I hissed, "Don't move!" Bill froze, but continued to puddle the ground in front of him.

The birds made a close-in pass just beyond him and we fired and a nice drake tumbled. The burly Lab who had been watching the whole thing with unbounded interest broke from the blind like a power fullback, clipped Bill neatly, and sent him sprawling into the reeking muck. We, of course, laughed immoderately.

The first time I met Bill was on a duck hunt. I knocked on the door of his camper and as it opened, I stuck out my hand to shake and introduce myself. Instead of a hand-shake, I found myself holding a beer. For the next nearly thirty years, Bill and I shared many a beer and many an adventure.

I hit him in the back of the head with a canoe pole on his first Ozark canoe trip. I had been looking at a lissome lovely in a nearby canoe and ran into the bank and lost my balance. I threw the pole to clear Bill's head and jumped out of the canoe, only to surface and see him bobbing up and down, his foot caught under the seat, half-dazed, half-drowned.

Turned out I hadn't thrown the pole *over* his head, but right into it, stunning him. And his supposedly waterproof gear bag wasn't, so he spent the night by the campfire, waiting for his sleeping bag to dry out.

Despite that inauspicious beginning we remained close friends. We hiked a northwest Missouri wildlife area in a snowstorm and camped in about ten inches of snow. An unlovely hound visited and made friends with Bill (or vice versa—he was a sucker for dogs). We shot pheasants, quail, and an incautious low-flying snow goose the next day.

We bicycled through Squaw Creek National Wildlife Refuge, Bill and his wife, Charlotte (who was never anything but "Charley" or "Char" to Bill). We canoed on the Gasconade and Bill forgot to close his camera box and tipped over, ruining several hundred dollars of equipment, but not his good nature, which was unruinable.

Bill was the outdoor editor for the *St. Joseph Gazette* and was inordinately proud of northwest Missouri. You could trash the rest of Missouri, but don't say anything bad about the Pony Express corner or he'd be all over you. He began as a photographer for the paper but loved the outdoors and saw that there was no coverage, so he volunteered to do a column. He knew newspapering and, with a reporter's curiosity, it wasn't long until he knew conservation and the mechanics of the outdoors, not just the results.

I was working for the Missouri Department of Conservation and every so often Bill would write a column that took yards of hide off the department. "He's your buddy," the brass would say. "Can't you do something about it?"

"First of all, it wouldn't do any good because I don't own Bill and neither does anyone else," I'd say. "Second, I wouldn't if I could because I respect him too much. And third, we probably deserved whatever he said."

But Bill also was a fierce defender of the department and Missouri's natural resources. He was no sycophant. He owed allegiance to the resource, not to this faction or that, and for that he earned the respect of readers and, over the years, even of those he had criticized.

Well, most of them anyway—once a conservation commissioner who had been skewered asked a photographer from the *Gazette* if he knew Bill Bennett. "Sure," the photog said.

"Well," said the commissioner, "if you see him, tell him to go screw himself."

I said, "Bill, you ought to nail him to the barn door."

"Naah," Bill said. "I don't want to descend to his level."

We spent many hours talking conservation and he did his homework. He went to workshops, served on citizen

committees, attended professional meetings, and, most of
all, hung around with wildlifers, picking their brains,
something that almost no outdoor columnist does. He realized that conservation was the bedrock on which hunting and fishing is based.

Many of our outings were far from formal. Once we
camped at Squaw Creek National Wildlife Refuge and had
a party with the area manager that night and watched his
Labrador do party tricks. Then the next morning we
hunted ducks and watched the Lab do what Labs are supposed to do—retrieve ducks. But we both learned more
about the politics, policies, and philosophies of the Fish
and Wildlife Service than we could have any other way.

There was the time that Bill took his young bird dog to
a farm and, as Bill was chatting with the farmer, the dog
attacked the farmer's chickens. Thinking to make a point,
Bill grabbed a chicken and beat the dog with it. Then he
discovered that, while the beating educated the dog, it
killed the chicken. "We was plannin' to butcher next
week," the farmer said. "Why don't you come back and
we'll make a sport of it."

For years Bill had a cable TV outdoor show. Once a
friend was a guest and was unusually quiet. Finally Bill, in
an attempt to draw him out, said, "You're sure quiet
today."

Then the guest, who had set up this practical joke with
the television crew, said, "Ah, I didn't want to be on this
bleeping show anyway," got up, and walked off.

And Bill shouted after him, "You can't say 'bleeping'
on television!" They still show the tape at parties.

Bill loved to bluegill fish with a fly rod more than anything on earth. A favorite memory is of him in a belly
boat late one evening paddling around a northwest Missouri lake, singing "The Wabash Cannonball" and casting
for his beloved fish.

Bill and Charlotte finally retired and Bill took up raising goats for no reason other than perhaps their cantan-
kerous nature appealed to him. He built a tiny little pond
and situated a tiny little camper trailer beside it. This was
where he relaxed with an accumulation of stray dogs and
the occasional goat.

When he wasn't there, he was in his "shop," a cluttered
office and workroom. Charlotte found Bill dead there,
with his feet propped up, a peanut in his hand and, I suspect, a beer close by. They had been married less than a
month short of forty-nine years. Bill was sixty-eight.

It was, as his daughter Yvonne said, a peaceful way to
go. And yet it was far too soon for the chubby, jolly little
guy whom I once dubbed "the northwest Missouri pixie,"
a nickname that haunted him the rest of his life.

Spence is still around. Although he groans more
than he once did, he still deserves the nickname we
gave him: the Iron Man. Spence has generated more
copy for me in thirty years than any other human. He
is a walking anecdote.

There was the time he felt a crushing natural urge and
dropped his drawers in a small ravine, modestly concealed
from his fellow hunters . . . but not from his bird dogs. As
Spence finished and rose to rearray himself, he didn't realize one of his dogs was busily rolling in the mess.

Spence's setters have provided enough memorable moments for a book by themselves, especially the episode with the chocolate-covered raisins. He was driving a venerable Volvo wagon and, like its owner, it was never quite fastened. The hatch wouldn't stay up, but Spence fixed that with a chunk of wood which he wedged between the floorboard and the hatch.

It was somewhat like toying with a hair-trigger guillotine every time you leaned into the back end for something. I lost a buck knife in the detritus and, search as I might, never could find it. Spence finally traded the machine for a pickup. Not long ago we got to talking about old times and I brought up the Volvo. "It's still running somewhere," he said with the faith of religion.

On a pheasant hunt a couple of years ago, we came back to the vehicles at day's end, chilled, weary, and ready for a hot shower and a cold drink. "We have a problem," Spence announced, ignoring the fact that *he* had the problem. "The truck keys are either locked inside or back on the nightstand at the motel."

They were inside the truck. My son-in-law, Ron De-Valk, is spiritual kin to the tinkerers who invented the machines that spawned the Industrial Age. Within minutes he had bent a shotgun cleaning rod into a crazy quilt of angles that allowed him to snake it through the window and flip the locking button off.

Later, I mounted the cleaning rod on a wooden plaque with a plate that read "Spence Turner Truck Key." I prepared to present it at a meeting. But a few days before the meeting Spence nipped the end off one of his fingers when a boat trailer came down on it. I sighed and made a trip to the nearest novelty shop for a rubber severed finger, which I mounted on the same plaque with another plate reading, "Spence Turner Boat Latch."

Ah, I love him.

I've been blessed with good hunting buddies. Foster Sadler was the best of them. He taught me just about all I know. He was my friend through the last couple of years of grade school, all through high school and for many years thereafter.

Foster should have been a bird dog. He hunted like one, ranging far, like a bony old pointer, on long legs and indefatigable energy. I would come to the hunting shack at day's end, tottering with crotch grab and knee sprain, and Foster would be as fresh as he had been at sunrise. We roamed many hills together, shooting at little brown birds. Then Foster took a dark road that I wasn't ready to travel.

Dave Mackey first took me on a quail hunt behind his setter when we were virtual youngsters, new in our professions. That was nearly thirty years ago. We've stumbled through the predawn turkey woods together, shivered in a sleet-stained deer blind . . . and walked countless miles after quail.

Dave is my reality check on the problems and possibilities of agriculture. His farm is a model of wildlife management, and he even somehow manages to raise a bumper crop of morel mushrooms each spring.

The Mackey extended family holds a barbecue contest each turkey season. It's not any old backyard soiree, but a major league gathering of master chefs, some of whom regularly enter state, regional, and national barbecue contests.

We sit on folding chairs under the basketball goal at Tim Schrage's place and drool while the ribs, pork butts, chicken, shrimp, and other exotica of the grill slowly smoke-cook to perfection. Tim is married to Dave's daughter, Beth.

The contest has grown from a few turkey hunters to a community affair of nearly a hundred. Tim and Beth's shorthair paces in his kennel downwind from the barbecuers, drool hanging from his chops.

I can't imagine not sprawling in a chair on a hot spring day, drooling in harmony with the dog—this is partly what friendship is. You see a couple of old codgers on a bench in front of the general store (or you would if there was a general store anymore) and they spit 'n' whittle and allow as how the weather ain't as hot (or as cold) as it used to be and that's probably because of the atom bomb.

But most of the time they just sit and you wonder what they possibly could be getting out of it. Being together, that's what. Being with a friend who doesn't judge and who doesn't have to be courted or convinced or coerced, who is just there.

Thereness is a priceless element of friendship.

Andy, my youngest son, has been hanging around with me since he was five. He's going on thirty-something now, with his own double, his own bird dogs, and his own life . . . but much of that life involves me as a friend.

He went with me to a duck camp, scarcely out of toddlerhood. The overheated old farmhouse sweated with outrageous stories and deliciously nasty language and I would see Andy's little synapses sparking and knew that he was storing information faster than an RDRAM memory module.

That he still hangs around with me, knowing what he does about my flaws and faults, is the measure of his friendship. Only this morning we hunted ducks together, as we often do.

It's a modest wetland pool that is off the flyway and only attracts the occasional duck or two, but it's convenient and no one else hunts there. We set out twenty duck decoys and a half dozen Canada goose decoys and sat on buckets thirty feet apart, behind a thin screen of weeds. Sometimes when one or the other is too lazy to make the trip, the other goes alone, but it isn't the same. We don't talk, other than the occasional comment about hearing turkeys fly down or a whispered, "There's a bunch high." But we aren't there to talk; just knowing that the other is close by is enough. It's shared pleasure, plus the shared pain of slogging through the predawn with a heavy sack of decoys, wading in the sucking mud of the pond, shivering in the cold.

Two wood ducks swung wide over the pond and then headed into the decoys and splashed down so quickly we didn't have time to raise our guns. "Let's get 'em!" I said, first words spoken in an hour. We rose and each killed a duck as they sprang into flight. Then, without words, we began picking up our decoys, each knowing what went in his tote sack.

I guess I lucked out with Andy because there was no choice—he's family. That he also is a best friend is a bonus. You check hunting buddies carefully, like used cars. They may have hidden faults—rust underneath or clanks in the transmission. It takes a bunch of driving to judge mules, used cars, and hunting buddies.

Some years back I courted a guy I thought would be a wonderful addition to my circle of hunting buddies. He was charming, funny, and intelligent. He knew bird hunting and talked a tough game.

He was a sham. He threw away friends like handi-wipes. Once three of us were quail hunting. My Brittany, Chip, went on point just as I happened over the hill. Mr. X was behind the point (he did have a facility for finding the action) and he didn't see me at the top of the hill.

It's accepted that if a dog is on point you holler "point!" and wait for your buddies to share in the action. Mr. X carefully looked around, didn't see me watching him, decided he had the point all to himself (with my dog), and flushed the birds.

I showed myself and asked how come he hadn't let us know the dog was pointing. "Oh, I was going to," he said. "But the dog bumped the birds and I had to shoot."

On another hunt, Andy was a green kid with a new gun, out with the big people for the first time. It was late afternoon and he hadn't shot. He'd been out of position on every flush. Now he was off to one side as Chip pointed in front of my erstwhile friend.

"Hang on," I said. "Let Andy get a shot." Andy trotted down the hill. Mr. X was just behind Chip and he very deliberately stepped forward, flushed the covey, and shot.

"The dog was going to bump them," he said, though the dog hadn't moved. Andy and I walked out of the field and went home. Today, many years later, Andy hunts with me. Mr. X has moved on to shed a couple of wives and a few more people who considered him a friend.

I hope there are few like him, but it seems that everyone I talk to has known someone like that. Perhaps there is a subculture of such users, living like alligators in the sewage system. They forget to pay their share of the expenses on a hunting trip. I thought it was carelessness or absentmindedness, except it kept happening.

And somehow I always busted the brush while Mr. X walked the perimeter and picked off easy shots. I'd do the dishes in a hunting shack while he was funny and charming to guests. I gritted my teeth, elbow deep in soapsuds. It took a while because I kept finding excuses for what he did (or didn't do), but finally it sank in.

He took advantage of everyone, really didn't care about anyone else. If it didn't benefit him in some way, it wasn't worth doing. He didn't forget—he just figured friends were disposable.

I've developed a set of commandments on the treatment of hunting buddies. I didn't go to a mountaintop where they were engraved on stone, though I've slipped and slid up and down a few mountains with my hunting buddies and in doing so have found these precepts. You walk a thousand miles through brush country, swamps, and prairies with people who matter and you come by some mutual criteria for judging who is a friend and who isn't . . . and how to treat them.

Here is what you do:

1. Buy your buddy's lunch some time for no good reason.
2. Remember his birthday and get him a scurrilous card that will make him laugh. Present it in front of your mutual friends. I'm saving one for Spence that reads, "When I get as old as you I hope like hell I smell a lot better."
3. Praise his dogs.
4. If you double on a bird, you say, "Nice shot!"
5. If you travel together, you pay 50 percent of the mutual costs and it wouldn't hurt to volunteer a little extra. Buy a round in a cowboy bar and say, "You get the next one," even if there is no next one.
6. If you promise something, bankrupt yourself, sell your kids, do whatever you have to do, to make sure you fulfill the promise.
7. Ask his advice on things. He probably is smarter than you anyway.
8. Laugh at his stories and jokes, especially the ones you've heard five times before.
9. Don't complain about him behind his back. We all have faults and you are not God's chosen messenger to point them out.
10. If he screws up, forgive him. If he hurts your feelings, let him know—chances are he didn't realize it and will feel awful. Grudges are postcards from hell.

There are ten commandments here because ten is a well-known commandment total, but there are many more. It boils down to accepting your hunting partners like your mate—for better or worse.

Phonies like Mr. X are mean and self-centered and should be no one's hunting buddy. Because hunting buddies are tolerant of each other, it may take a long time for a rift to develop, but ultimately the Mr. X's of the world find themselves running the ridges alone. They are true lone wolves. They can't possibly be content like that and perhaps that is their ultimate punishment, to travel alone with the knowledge that no one who matters cares about them.

I don't know who wrote the following. It was on the Internet, forwarded so many times that its source has vanished. But it's such a neat little summation of both buddies and dogs that it's worth forwarding one more time.

Consider this . . .

If you can start the day without caffeine, if you can get along without pep pills, if you can always be cheerful, ignoring aches and pains, if you can resist complaining and boring people with your troubles, if you can eat the same food every day and be grateful for it, if you can understand when your loved ones are too busy to give you any time, if you can overlook it when those you love take it out on you when, though no fault of yours, something goes wrong, if you can take criticism and blame without resentment, if you can ignore a friend's limited education and never correct him/her, if you can resist treating a rich friend better than a poor friend, if you can face the world without lies and deceit, if you can conquer tension without medical help, if you can relax without liquor, if you can sleep without the aid of drugs, if you can honestly say that deep in your heart you have no prejudice against creed, color, religion, or politics:

Then, my friend, You are ALMOST as good as your dog.

TWELVE

The Sum of Our Days

So many of them are gone, eye blinks in time and remembered mostly by me.

Britt, the first of them, who set an example that his successor, Chip, did not profit by—both were killed by automobiles, the most efficient predator of the erstwhile pointing spaniel.

Then there was Ginger, Chip's phantom lover, who lured him in front of that Detroit juggernaut with her in-season spoor, Ginger, who wanted to talk so badly, perhaps to tell me tales of her wild adventures. She would look earnestly into my eyes and her mouth would move as if she were desperately trying to form words, but only doggy moans came forth.

It must have been frustrating for her as I urged her to keep trying: "Come on, Ginger. I know you can do it if only you try hard enough." And she would fix me with those alien yellowish eyes and seek to break through the physiological barrier that made her unable to say, "You ain't gonna believe where I was last night!"

And Guff lies on the hill across the pond, his spirit keeping watch on his sprawling family as they sport in the water or slide on the ice in a frantic game of dog tag. Perhaps his daughter Pepper is somewhere nearby.

I can imagine her gathering herself as Death approached, only to find that it was the one entity in her long life that she couldn't stare down with The Look.

And there are the ones still alive as I wind up their stories, Dacques still with the poster dog looks that made him the heartthrob of many a bitch, but now grayed and beset by arthritis, his hobbyhorse gallop slowed to a painful hobble.

And Chubby, my faithful sleep toy, who apparently has the power to heal—at least he has made me feel better when he nestled close to me when I was sick.

It's a new year, a new century, a new millennium. But no matter how we ignore it, inevitably old dogs and old hunters go creaky. Once I took Andy one-on-one in basketball and beat him every time. Now I groan with the effort of a game of Horse.

The years roll along and Time is a grouchy old bastard with no compassion. It came home to roost a couple of years ago for Spence Turner. Spence's father had been in a nursing home for many months and for the past few days his body had been shutting down. It was a matter of time. Spence knew it.

He just didn't know it was a matter of so little time. My father died more than thirty years ago. He was at the center of my life for all my years. He took me fishing and hunting and put the love of each in my heart. He was, as all fathers are to all youngsters, an eternal presence.

His father had been the same for him, teaching much by example and not a little bit by necessity. My father grew up on a hard-rock Chariton County, Missouri, hill farm with all the necessities, but no luxuries.

While shooting squirrels or rabbits was undeniably fun, it also was part of stocking the cupboard. Same with fishing. My grandfather, a carpenter, was a craftsman at construct-ing fish traps that were as effective as they were illegal.

He didn't pass along his outlaw tendencies to my father, but the joy of catching a fish ran deep. My father married a northwoods girl from Birchwood, Wisconsin, a small resort town, and I split my growing up between farm life in Mis-souri and the deep lake waters of the northwoods.

The outdoors infused my blood from both sides of the family. For both my parents, the outdoors was more than an avocation or recreation; it was a presence and at times an enemy. They'd lived off it, avoided its perils, and learned to enjoy it.

My aunt, then fourteen years old, watched the local sawbones (a literal name) saw off her brother's leg on the kitchen table. The leg had been crushed by a falling tree. Life was tough then, and few families escaped sibling death.

You had a bunch of brothers and sisters, but they were trimmed off like quail covey mates, here taken by a preda-tor, there felled by disease. Whooping cough and diphthe-ria and scarlet fever weren't historic citations; they were as real as the sunset.

Once my father took his father north to Birchwood, Wisconsin, and they caught strange fish that you'd never see in the muddy streams of north Missouri. My grandfather hooked and landed a sizable northern pike. Before my father could shout a warning, the old man stuck his hand in the pike's jaw to wrestle his spoon loose. The pike raked half the skin off his hand with its many teeth.

When my grandfather lay dying of a stroke, nearly eighty years old, my father surely recalled that moment in an old wooden boat on a conifer-scented northern lake. He never forgot that sad deathwatch in the little farmhouse down in the hills, but he would not have dwelled on that. No, he would have remembered a dear old man with a brushy white mustache and a crinkly smile and a hand that looked as if it had gone through a meat grinder.

As time passes, you remember the good times, not ebbing life and the stillness of death. You really don't rid yourself of the awfulness of death; you just put it in a dusty cupboard and hope no one opens the latch. Sometimes, in the dark of the night, the doors pop open for a moment or two, but then you think of days in the squirrel woods or sunrises over a duck marsh, and the cupboard doors swing shut again.

And I don't forget my father's long hospital stay, the worsening physical condition, the call just at suppertime, telling me he had died. I knew he was deathly ill, knew it was coming, but it was like the death of Spence's father—expected but not expected. I cried, just as Spence did. "I didn't realize I'd take it so hard," Spence said.

And I hadn't either, but death is a finality. As long as there is breath, there is a slender thread of hope, even if you know there is no hope. Then when the news comes, it is the end of a life shared. There will be no new memories created.

My memories now are of days in the squirrel woods with my father and a dog, now also long gone. Chaps was nominally my dog, but her heart belonged to her squirrel woods buddy. She and my father would vanish into the Bend, a pocket of tall bottomland timber on the old Chariton River channel, and come back a few hours later with several squirrels.

Chaps treed them; my father shot them with a Winchester single-shot .22 that would drive nails at fifty yards—still will, because I now use it in my squirrel woods and I know it will shoot where you point it.

Guns and fishing rods are only part of the legacy. My turkey gun is a Model 12 Winchester, silvered by the rasp of work-roughened hands. It belonged to my father. Guns endure, people don't.

The memories are as enduring as the machined parts and slick action of the old Model 12. Maybe there's a bit of soul in that cold metal and darkened wood. I know Winchester couldn't build soul into its guns, but the sweat-stained walnut and the silvered receiver are the evidence of use, the memento of users. Something other than sweat surely soaked into that wood, dissolved the bluing on that receiver, some essence of the loved one who carried it.

You think maybe your father never will die as long as his gun is in use. You can look at a father's death as the end of everything or you can look at it as a phase, from which you go on with a different set of rules. I like the lat-ter—the idea that my father still is in the duck blind with me, in his old gun, in my mind, in my memories.

Ted woke us before dawn in the cabin by the river. He did it with an Irish drinking toast and we laughed and rubbed at our gritty eyes. We loaded the Explorer with de-coys, Jet the Lab, guns, and ourselves. We watched the headlights bob and weave down rutted country roads through the silent northwoods.

We walked down a grassy hill in the moonless predawn and glimpsed water shining ahead. Ted slid his duck boat into the marsh and distributed a dozen or so decoys. They squatted in the still water, motionless and lifeless. You need a little chop to give decoys life; these had none. But so what. We inhaled the dawn and loved where we were and what we were doing.

The rising sun touched the decoys and the aspens glowed. A snipe skittered through the morning light, like an arrowhead without the shaft behind it. Its rusty-hinge call trailed behind.

No one raised a gun. By the time we'd identified it as a legal game bird, it was gone and no one rued that we didn't get a shot. It was a skittery exclamation point to a perfect dawn. This dawn was so perfect it could only reaffirm life.

We sat on stumps or log chunks dredged from the marsh grass. It was moderate cold, not enough to be un-comfortable. You couldn't help but believe in life renew-ing if you watched the glow of the trees and the coppery sheen of the water. You felt as if you could live forever . . . if only you didn't think about it.

There was no phone in the cabin, only at Ted's house up the hill. So if news were to come it would come to Ted, not to us. "Since it was a day he'd remember for the rest of his life, I tried to make it as right as possible," Ted said.

Ted began to talk to Spence in a low voice and I could barely hear him. "I want you to remember how the world looks at this moment," Ted said. "The sun coming up, the trees turning, everything about it." There was a long silence while Spence did just that and, I think, began to realize what Ted was getting at. "I got a call early this morning," Ted said. We all knew then. We knew that Spence's life as he had known it for all his years was irrevocably changed, that his father's life was ended.

Spence said nothing. Then he opened his gun and withdrew the shells, went up the hill, and released his bird dogs from their pickup kennel. He puttered with the dogs, using them as a balance, a link to normalcy. I waited a few minutes to let him do whatever he had to do, then went up the hill, stiffly as if I were not quite awake. This is a man with whom I have shared the best and the worst of the outdoors for thirty years.

He and I have watched each other get grizzled and gray and gimpy. We've buried friends and dogs and known good times and bad. This was bad. There are no words, only the presence of someone who cares. I hugged him and we stood wordlessly. I wished for magic phrases that you say to your best friend that will ease the pain, but there are none. All you can do is be there, feeling awkward and insufficient.

Spence and I both have sons who hunt and each is see-ing his Old Man become an old man. Now Spence and I sweat and my back seizes and spasms and Spence's ankles strain against the yards of tape he applies in the early hours.

We'd been hunting out of the sagging cabin on Pine River for fifteen years. Heavy rains put dimples in the var-nished ceiling inside and Ted scratched his head one year and wondered aloud if the cabin was worth a new roof. Spence and I looked at him as if he were wondering if the Declaration of Independence was worth preserving from the National Archives mice. The kids started coming to the cabin after we'd put in a dozen years getting it just right.

Andy, my youngest son and hunting buddy, became Tall Hunting Andy to Ted's six-year-old daughter, Molly, who hoped she would grow up and marry this lanky prince from Missouri. Mac is Spence's youngest son, gone off to be a computer genius, but returned to his dad's roots as a hunter.

You don't like to think about it, but someday one might stand awkwardly while the other is silent, shoulder-ing a terrible misery. Young dogs replace old ones, young hunters replace old ones, and there is a new crop of birds for each. Life feeds on death and nature is eternal.

It's not what we want, but it's what we get. And the good times become faded photos and entries in hunting di-aries and a turn in the trail where you once were with someone who is not there now.

For Andy that someone was Brian Schmidt, a friend and hunting buddy since they were in grade school. Brian was almost home when he lost control of his pickup. Brian

was killed. He was twenty-nine. He had a whole life
ahead. Twenty-nine is just a kid. That's how I thought
of him. Of course, to me just about everyone is a kid. I remember when Andy and Brian's voices started to change,
when they began to drive.

I think of the many years Brian never will have, the
thirty-four more years I have lived that he never will. And
it seems such a waste of a vital natural resource—a young
hunter and angler.

Our local high schools have hundreds of students, but
relatively few ever are in the field with a gun or rod. Fewer
still own bird dogs. Brian and Andy were exceptions. They
shared all the fun that any friends share, but in addition
they shared experiences in the woods and the fields and
on the water. They each owned and trained bird dogs and
loved nothing better than to see those dogs do everything
right, to find and hold birds. They shared in the covey
flush and the fluster of shots.

Andy and I hunted with Brian near the end of the
quail season on his farm in a bend of the Osage River. It
was a gray, cold day, and the quail season in Missouri
needed to improve to be called miserable. A one-covey
day was the norm and there were plenty of hunts where it
wasn't even that good.

"There's at least four coveys on the place," Brian said.
"And maybe more." The house he shared with his wife of
a year sits atop a ridge, overlooking the Osage River valley.
The bottom was a checkerboard of small fields, corn, grass,
beans, interspersed with woody ditches and fencerows.
Ideal quail habitat.

Brian let his two bird dogs loose and we added a couple of ours. Brian had good knowledge of quail management and he put it to use on his farm. He knew where the birds should be and, sure enough, they were there when the dogs cruised through. We talked quail management and couldn't know that the boy who had grown up with our son, who had always come out on top in the hunting competition, was near the end of his life.

The dogs bumped the first covey, but we got some shooting on scatters. It was a day of mixed dog work— some good, some not. But we had plenty of shooting and killed several birds each. It was the most productive hunt of the season. We found four coveys in a couple of hours. It was the best hunt of the season beyond the finding of birds. It was good because the two friends were together and I got to share in that friendship.

They were outdoor kids. Brian was more successful at it because he had more room to roam; the family farm had many deer and turkeys and quail. Each year it seemed Andy would come close on a big gobbler, but Brian would kill one.

He kidded Andy but it was gentle ribbing with no malice, and Andy never was jealous of Brian's success. They stayed friends and would talk about the upcoming season. Andy always was going to kill the Boss Gobbler . . . and Brian did.

Year after year Andy worked harder than I did at turkey hunting and for all the reasons you can think of it didn't pan out. He lost one that he rolled in its tracks, only to see the tough old gobbler shake it off and run away. We tracked the bird, like a shot deer, for more than half a mile until it reached dry ground and we lost it.

Andy bought a turkey gun with an extra full choke and a three-inch chamber. No bird hit square could survive. But he shot another one that flopped sideways and then leaped up and when Andy shucked a second cartridge, his face mask rode up and blinded him and the bird escaped.

It was like that. Brian would kill a twenty-pound-plus gobbler and Andy would have only another story of misfortune, birds that came to his call at angles impossible for him to shoot or were behind a screen of brush or that stayed just out of gun range.

Andy got the news about Brian on Sunday morning, the day before the Missouri turkey season opener. Brian and he had talked earlier about how the season would go, and I'm sure there was little doubt in Brian's mind that he would nail a big gobbler. He always did.

Andy could have stayed home the next morning, grieving, but he didn't think Brian would have wanted that. Andy didn't say it, but I think the turkey hunt was a tribute to his friend and certainly an escape from grief. Andy went to the edge of our property on Sunday evening, called, and got an immediate response. He crawled out of the woods on hands and knees, sure that the gobbler would follow the call into our woods and be there opening morning. And so it was.

"I was putting on my britches at a quarter of six when I heard him gobble," Andy says. The rest was almost anticlimax. Andy slipped around to the glade, set a couple of decoys, listened to the gobbler fly down, and called it past him within a half dozen feet. The big bird fluffed its feathers audibly as it passed my son and drifted in front of him and he killed the first turkey of his hunting life. It weighed twenty-two pounds and had a 10½-inch beard and ¾-inch spurs. It was a bragging bird.

The next night Andy went to the funeral home. There were photos of Brian and turkeys and deer he'd taken, and there was one of Andy and Brian. "It must have been back in the seventh grade," Andy said. "I was wearing a stupid blue jacket that I don't even remember and we were together. And there were all those pictures of Brian with turkeys and he always kidded me about not getting one. Now I got one and I can't tell him about it."

Was it coincidence that Andy killed his first turkey on the first opening day in years that his longtime friend would not be in the woods? Should Andy grieve because the two of them can't share his success? Or should he believe that this coincidence is something more impenetrable, that a torch has been passed back from one friend to another from somewhere down a dark and steep road?

So many memories are cloudy with the pain of separation. But counterbalancing that is the sunshine of the good days. Once Andy wasn't big enough to lift a shotgun. He hunted at heel, like a retriever, and held the little brown birds I shot nestled in his hand as he stroked them. Then came the day that he went four-for-five on quail with his Browning double and griped because he missed one shot. He doesn't miss often.

Time was I shot more birds in a day than he did. But one day he had four birds, I had two . . . and was glad to get them. We won't discuss how many of my shots were involved.

Time was Andy wasn't old enough to drive a car and couldn't have seen over the steering wheel anyway. Then one day I drove us down a dirt road to a low waterhole that looked impassable. "I'll take it through," he said. I considered my pride briefly, then muttered, "Okay, but you walk for the tractor to haul us out." He slicked the Suburban through the hole without even racing the engine.

Time was . . .

I remember a day a couple of years ago. The old dogs still were able to go long hours, including this old dog, but we all paid for it in sore muscles and weariness that took a while to go away. It was dark and snow was falling as we quit and I was tired to the bone. Andy was tired too, but not as tired as I because he isn't packing around all those years and miles, all that abraded, degraded old-rubber cartilage and sinew and bone and skin.

He's tomorrow and I'm almost yesterday. Some fathers want their sons to become congressmen or other dregs of society; all I ever wanted was that Andy become a quail hunter and, more specifically, my hunting buddy. He has done both of his own volition.

Once there was a television commercial in which a fatherly looking type turns to a fresh-faced kid and says, "Take her through, son," and the kid guides them through a whitewater rapids while a background singer wails, "He's a maaaaaan!" as if his vitals were being clawed by catamounts.

It was a rite of passage as viewed by Madison Avenue. I forget what they were selling, but it was something you and your kid could share, like a Porsche or underarm deodorant that smells like a stock saddle.

Andy and I don't need to buy things to share experiences. We don't need to sing about it either. Or even talk about it. We don't backpat each other and glow with familial pride. We just have a good time together, comfortable, like two old codgers who always know where the other one is and who share shots and laughs.

On the day I'm remembering Andy is writing in his gunning diary and I hope there is a bit of charity for the old man who used to be the young man. I think he's proud of me, though he'd never admit it. He doesn't go around bragging about his dad, but I know he thinks it's neat to have a father who loves to take him to the sloughs and marshes and foxtail meadows and cobbly frozen crop fields.

Our dogs pointed three of the five coveys we found and each dog assumed the point position once, while the others acted as honor guard. I trained two of the dogs but Andy trained Dacques, the one most likely to find birds. He worked with the stout puppy though all the trauma of obedience training, then honed his inborn skills. Dacques has always been a meat dog.

Our five hours resulted in abraded skin, quivering muscles, wind-chapped faces, and a rat cheese and ham sandwich at a little crossroads mom-and-pop grocery store in a town charmingly named Hedge City, population about four.

"It's *real* ham," the proprietress said proudly. It tasted like real ham as imagined by someone who'd never seen a pig, but it filled. "We been here since 1932. I built this place myself," said the husband. "There's a bench over there. Take a seat." Instead I perched on a stack of pop cases and listened to the history of the store.

Andy will remember this store one day the way I remember the Guilford Ford hardware store where my father bought me a Red Ryder BB gun. Once I pinned the neighbor's kid in the family outhouse, rattling BBs off the walls while he squalled for his mother . . . who then proceeded to whale the daylights out of me. It was a lesson in gun safety never forgotten.

Andy and I hunted a series of wooded draws, separated by pasture. Pasture often is a curse for quail. Fescue is a grass so vile for bird hunters that it must have grown first in a particularly dismal corner of hell. But this was Reed's canary grass, with some lespedeza and foxtail mixed in. That combination first sprouted in a sweet corner of heaven.

The birds were nestled at the bottom of the draw, cupped in the hand of the woods. They're always there, inches from salvation, for once they flit into the woods, they become ruffed grouse, except not as big. They jink through the dark trees, as elusive as leprechauns.

But some inevitably overfly the woods and scatter on the far hill and it is there that the old house stands. That house too has had its time. Andy and I climbed the hill to the angular, abandoned building.

The house is surrounded by tall prairie grass and it overlooks a sweep of country you might expect on the western plains. It's an atypical house for north Missouri,

not quite a mansion but much more than a sagging clap-
board farmhouse.

It's at least a hundred years old and no one has lived in
it for more than twenty years. The last inhabitants were just
caretakers, orderlies monitoring the death of a patient that
had lived beyond its time. They lived in it but didn't love it.

The ones who loved it are almost forgotten. Andy and
I circled the house, ostensibly looking for the scattered
quail, but really lost in our own thoughts about the old
house. People of flesh and bone and pity and love lived
there long before I was born, and the memory of them is as
dim as the gray, paintless siding.

This was an elegant house, planned for hosting parties
and reflecting the pride of those who lived there. Two
rows of century-old eastern red cedars lined a walkway
from the front stoop to . . . where? There is no sign of a
road, nor lane. The walk merely stops twenty yards from
the porch as if those who walked it entered another di-
mension when they came to the end.

The bird dogs were untouched by the mystery of the
grand house so far from anyone else, so far from a road.
They coursed the prairie, looking for scatters. Dogs refine
life to its essentials. Birds and then more birds.

Presently, Dacques slowed, tensed, and pointed, and
Andy and I became what we were before we became
philosophers—hunter/gatherers. Never mind the old house
and its secrets; quail were crouched in the prairie grass and
the dog was down on them.

We walked into the point and a single rose into the
morning light and I didn't shoot. The boy/man tumbled

the bird into the Indian grass and his dog pounced on it and brought it home to Andy's hand.

So now I'm writing in my diary and Andy in his. Maybe it's silly, and almost certainly it is pointless to ponder on the lost times. The good times are now, not then. The little boy Andy is as gone as those who lived in the old house, but the man Andy spent time with his dad on a north Missouri knoll where there were dogs and quail.

There was a time, sure. But more important, there *is* a time and it is now.

About the Author

Joel Vance is owned by seven French Brittanies at last count.

He and his patient wife Marty live on forty acres along a dead-end gravel road in central Missouri where the dogs can chase squirrels and rabbits and ignore shouted commands.

Vance recognizes two seasons of the year: bird season and thinking about bird season.

Vance wrote for the Missouri Conservation Department for more than twenty years before his retirement and now writes columns for *Gun Dog* and *Wing and Shot* magazines, as well as a humor column for *North American Fisherman*.

He has been president of the Outdoor Writers Association of America and has been honored by all three of its major awards.

As for a personal philosophy, Vance says. "The older I get and the more I see what idiocies people are capable of, the more I admire bird dogs."